NO BARRIERS

NO BARRIERS

By
Neal Petersen

BROOKSIDE

Dublin

NO BARRIERS

First published in 1994 by

Brookside

2 Brookside

Dundrum Road

Dublin 14

ISBN 1 874597073

Cover design by Jon Berkeley.

Cover photo by Win de Koning

Typesetting by Graphic Resources.

Printed in Ireland

by Colour Books Ltd., Baldoyle.

*To Mom, Dad and my sister, Jan,
John Killeen, Gwen Wilkinson, and
to all my friends who helped make
my dreams come true.*

Contents

FOREWORD

OUR SURPRISE VISITOR:

Galway and Ireland was as surprised to welcome Neal Peterson as he was to arrive here from South Africa. It was courtesy of the Irish Naval Service who had towed the rudderless "Stella-r" into Galway Docks.

"Protect Our Sealife" was boldly flashed across the vessel's side. This mission statement reflected as much a lone life on board as it did the surrounding ocean.

It was an early Monday morning. I just happened to be there on board the Irish Ocean Racing and Youth Club Pride and was honoured to meet Neal. Our previous encounter was the previous year while attempting to demolish black porter, and dreaming dreams at the London Boat Show's Guinness stand.

By mid morning Jim Fahy had broadcast Neal's story nationwide on radio. My next memory is of John Killeen and the "lads" lunching in the Galway Arms. Swiftly they rallied to support the lone sailor and so began the next installment of the remarkable Neal Peterson story.

It is a story eloquently told in this book.

A delightful read, it reflects a fascinating tale of hardship, adventure, challenge and, above all else confronting the odds.

Even at the best of times to sail the ocean is tough. To do it alone is even tougher. Not only must you cook, navigate, steer, set sail and run your ship but you must stay "sane" as well for long periods of isolation.

If this was all Neal had to worry about, things would be okay. However to gather resources, money and support to get back together when you start with nothing is an even greater obstacle. Being black, before it was fashionable to be so in South Africa, was even tougher.

Not only must you be a sailor, you must be a salesman, builder, accountant and everything else while staying secure in your ambition and remaining distressingly sane .... Not only has Neal gone out and preached his message at those with money to raise funds but he has also visited prisons and related his adventures to those cut off from society, he has lectured youth groups and members of the travelling community.

This is why I am honoured to write this foreword. In a small way I know and can relate to what Neal has gone through to get to this stage and the formidable challenges that lie ahead for him. There is risk involved but it is one of choice. We all have day to day pressures, responsibilities but we need free spirits and adventurers like Neal Peterson.

And this is why I encourage you to not only sit back and enjoy this book but to identify with and support the enormous challenge and adventure involved.

Enda O'Coineen
Ireland,
25th March 1994

1

GROWING YEARS

It was in early June 1992 that I sailed my 38-foot yacht, *Stella-r*, across the Atlantic Ocean for the second time. Nearly midway between the two continents, fog engulfed my boat and became more dense. I could barely see three boat lengths ahead. I had first encountered the fog the previous day, two weeks after the start of the solo transatlantic race from Plymouth, on the south-west coast of England, to Newport, Rhode Island on the American east coast.

The water temperature was warm at sixteen degrees, but soon it became cooler. I was racing into the confluence of the Gulf Stream, where it merged with the Labrador current. I had chosen to sail a particular route to take advantage of the ocean currents.

Since leaving Plymouth I had pushed my racing yacht hard. As the *Stella-r* moved through the thick fog, I settled into an unchanging routine of a long snooze of two hours in the afternoon, with half-an-hour catnaps for the rest of the day. At sunrise and sunset, I would poke my head out of the hatch to look around me. The colours of the sky were not only beautiful; they could tell me a little about the weather that was to come.

I was always at my navigation table at 11:00 GMT to hear Portishead radio broadcast a weather bulletin and give the position of some of the yachts in the race on the high frequency radio. These reports were made on several different frequencies, which enabled the boats to receive information almost right across the Atlantic. Each day after the Portishead radio broadcast, I plotted my position from the navigation aid on a chart. Using dividers, I counted the miles left to the finish of the race and assessed what progress I had made in the previous twenty-four hours. On the day of which I am writing, I still had to sail some 1,350 miles before I could realise my childhood dream. Within three days I would be about 400 miles due west, in the shallow waters off the Grand Banks of Newfoundland.

The *Stella-r* was carrying full sail. The wind was out of the south, but it was not blowing hard. It looked possible to set the spinnaker, the large colourful racing sail used when the wind comes from astern of the beam. I watched the wind direction closely and decided to alter my course slightly to the north of my westerly heading so that I could fly the spinnaker, but I waited a while before making the course change. Then an hour later the wind direction changed. I went up on deck after my afternoon nap and set the colourful spinnaker. Down came the head sail and up it went.

The boat's speed climbed dramatically. I was pleased with my progress. A school of dolphins played around the bow as the *Stella-r* surfed off the following sea. I could hear their squeaks and squeals when I was below deck. When the daylight had vanished, they sped on, leaving me alone in the fog on a measureless ocean.

My progress had been good. The first light of another day found me eighty miles closer to Newport, but visibility was poor. I was tired, having taken only one half-hour nap during the hours of darkness. Since the wind had freshened, the boat speed increased, but the fog was as dense as ever. Then, suddenly, the water temperature dropped rapidly; within seven hours it fell from fifteen degrees to four degrees. The Labrador current had me in its grip. Soon, I knew, it would become a game of Russian roulette because there were icebergs ahead and I could hardly see where I was going. Throughout the day I felt apprehensive. I questioned whether I had made a mistake in sailing too far north. Portishead radio broadcast the positions of several competitors ahead of me, who were sailing a similar route to the one I had chosen. To sail west, but further south of my latitude, would increase their lead. All afternoon I worried about the possibility of hitting an iceberg, or going south-west and losing time. I chose to keep my course. After all, I was in a race and had to take calculated risks.

During the second night under spinnaker, I was below deck snoozing when I felt the boat beginning to move very sluggishly. I rushed up and was shocked to find that the spinnaker had gone. It was in the water being dragged ten feet astern. The halliard, a rope used to hoist or lower the sail, had chafed through and snapped. I spent a long time retrieving the spinnaker, pulling the wet sail hand over hand out of the water and being very careful not to tear it.

Because I had no other halliard, I set the genoa. This is a large triangular headsail. My speed fell significantly. I sat waiting for daybreak so that I could take stock of my situation. The dawn brought more wind and a larger swell, so I could not climb the mast to replace the halliard.

Two more days passed, and I was running before a lovely breeze, but I was frustrated because progress could have been better if the spinnaker had been set.

I waited until the wind died down. *Stella-r* and I had a disheartening night, sailing only 48 miles instead of her normal average of 65 miles. The sea settled and I gained enough courage to climb to the very top of the mast, the first time I had done this at sea single-handed. I prepared a two purchase block and tackle, hoisting it to the top of the mast on the genoa halliard. One end was tied to the bosun's chair. I hauled myself hand over hand to the first spreader, and rested. Then I went up to the second spreader. I began to feel weak and exhausted and was banged about against the mast as it scribed arcs in the sky when the gentle swell rocked the hull. Yet on I climbed and threaded what was left of the old halliard. At the top of the mast, with the boat heeling gently, I looked down at the water about fifty-five feet below, and shut my eyes tight.

Overcoming my fear to climb the mast while sailing on my own was no mean feat. When I got back on deck, my knees were wobbly, so I sat for a long time and thought about what I had achieved. I had unpleasant visions of a vessel finding my body entangled at the top of the mast, or splattered on the deck. Still, I had done it.

When the sun had set, I kept my boat sailing as fast as she would go. I had regained my composure, but it took several hours before I recovered fully. I was back in the race with my spinnaker set. Ahead lay what would be the greatest moment of my life, the finish. Newport, Rhode Island, the sailing capital of the world, where every three or four years sailing nations raced against the United States for the America's Cup.

Stella-r had carried me across the Atlantic. The race had been hard, but now her bow was slicing through the water, bringing me closer to the finishing line. I knew I was not going to win the race, but I had accepted the challenge. From childhood I had learnt to face up to the responsibility of overcoming whatever difficulties lay ahead.

***

Since my boyhood it had been my ambition to race solo across the Atlantic. My dream began in Cape Town, South Africa, lying in hospital when I was six, reading books on the sea. Books inspired me and helped me to escape from my hospital bed into the world of yachtsmen and yachtswomen who had accepted the sea's challenge.

I was born on the 3rd June 1967 with only one complete hip joint. As a small child I had spent a lot of time in hospital, undergoing operations and learning to walk. I could not run and kick a ball like other kids, but I found my niche in the water. It all began when I was seven years old and started water therapy learning to swim. Then when I was nine I became a sport diver.

14

Neal at home after his first operation

Dad had been a diver after the Second World War. He loved the sea, and taught me to snorkel and dive. He had earned his living diving for aberlone and crayfish, until 1958, when the South African government passed a law that made diving licences compulsory. Aberlone is a slow-growing shellfish that feeds on seaweed; it is found only around the southern South African coasts, and in certain Australian and Californian waters. Its very rich taste makes it a great delicacy.

Coloured men were not granted licences. Dad and his staff — three people — were cast aside. When he no longer could earn his living at sea, he took a job in a plastics manufacturing factory and found an escape for his disappointment in alcohol. His loss of what he truly loved taught me the value of having a dream and realising it. Nothing, I told myself, was going to stop me.

My mother was a schoolteacher who had taught me that education was the key to success. Accepting challenges and competing was the way to win. Finishing first was only a bonus. When I said one day that I wanted a yacht, she encouraged me to work for it. Without her, I would not have been able to accept the challenges of life.

Diving gave me freedom. My parents helped me to buy a wetsuit, but before that I used to dive in a bathing costume, with a cheap mask, fins and snorkel. The waters near Cape Town were cold all year round, but I kept hunting for aberlone and lobsters. Since we were recreational divers, no licence was required. I sold some of the fish I caught, saving the money for that wetsuit.

I did not get pocket money, but all my basic needs were provided for at home. The seafood that I did not sell, I contributed towards the family table. My mother made a donation towards my wetsuit. Eventually I saved up enough to buy a second-hand wetsuit which proved to be too large for me. I wore an old woollen jumper underneath it, and was able to spend longer in the water, gathering larger catches. Soon I was yearning to scuba dive.

I was an avid reader of books about the sea. I began reading books on sailing, mostly written by single-handed sailors who took up the quest to circumnavigate the globe. Francis Chichester wrote *A World of my Own*; Alex Rose wrote *Lively Lady*, but Bernard Moitessier's, *The Long Way* was the most fascinating. It was about the Frenchman's quest to sail solo non-stop around the world in 1968. Leading the race, after rounding Cape Horn, he questioned why he was prepared to give up his new-found peace for public notoriety. Instead, he sailed halfway around again, to settle in Tahiti.

One man, one boat. The exhilaration came from sending a vessel surfing down waves at thunderous speeds. It did not matter where the lone sailors came from, but where they dared dream to go, in search of adventure.

One Sunday my mother invited a school colleague over to tea. As the afternoon progressed, rain clouds swept in from the west. The colleague's boyfriend, Tony, asked to be excused: he was building a yacht and had left the cockpit open. I asked if I could go with him, and so became enthralled with my first yacht, a 43-foot sloop, *Blue Heron*. Afterwards, I went over regularly to where Tony had the

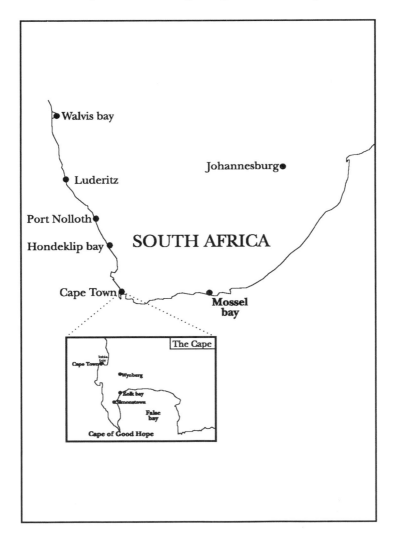

boat not very far from where we lived, to help him by cleaning the brushes he used for varnishing, and making coffee. Tony lent me several books on crewing and navigation.

When I was twelve, I started attending Livingstone High School, where my mother had been a pupil, and where she now taught. 1980 was a dreadful year for education in South Africa. There was a nationwide boycott of classes in most of the schools classified by the government as 'coloured schools'. It all began during the second term, before the important mid-year exams. The pupils held a referendum in most schools to decide whether or not to boycott class in protest at segregated education. The majority of pupils at Livingstone, regarded as a politically active and progressive school, voted in favour of boycotting classes.

I was against the boycott, reasoning that, without an education, we could not rule our country. However inferior it may be, education is the key to any freedom; it gives us the capacity to progress, and turn our ideas to fruition. Education is gained not only at school, but through growing up to discover life and to learn the daily lessons life teaches. Experience, travel, what my parents taught me and reading were a large part of my education. School laid a foundation for me to build upon. It did not begin when the bell rang in the mornings, nor did it end when the bell pealed at the end of the school day. My education was around me every moment of the day. Some students extended their knowledge of the world by going to university. Others took up apprenticeships. My education was enhanced through the life I chose to live.

At school some pupils shunned me for voicing my views. Many of the students who spoke in favour of the boycott were weak academically, and saw it as an opportunity to skip classes. The weeks passed and, although we went to school, there were no classes. We lost nine weeks of school.

18

I kept up my studies at home in the afternoons, with my mother guiding and encouraging me.

Weekends were a relief. Even though I put aside plenty of time for reading, I pursued other interests. Dad and I regularly went to sea aboard a Kalk Bay fishing boat. My sister, Jan, who is eight years older than me, had no interest in joining us, because she was prone to getting seasick. We would cast off from the harbour before daybreak, so that we could be at the fishing grounds by sunrise. Once there, we never stopped working and did not notice the time pass. Mostly we caught snoek, a fish indigenous to South African waters that is related to the barracuda. Since we were guests on board, we gave one-third of our catch to the boat, to contribute to running expenses. We normally took home about seven snoek, giving several away to friends.

Before long, I was asked to assist with certain jobs on board. I helped to haul in the anchor at the fishing grounds, and at the end of the day was taught to helm the boat, handing over the tiller only when we were just off the harbour. These activities helped to take my mind off the nausea I felt when I was on the water. Still, the spirit of adventure had gripped me and eventually the bouts of seasickness passed.

One weekend in March 1980, Dad and I drove the seven miles to Kalk Bay, only to find that the boats were not going to sea. The previous day's catch had been poor because of the low water temperature. Disappointed, we drove south another ten miles along the bay, to Simonstown, the naval harbour. Simonstown was a beautiful bay, lined by a mountain range, facing away from the south-west wind. Several yachts were bobbing in the bay, tugging at their moorings. As we drove past, I asked Dad if we could stop. Perhaps, I hoped, someone might take us sailing.

I walked along the slipway where people were launching dinghies, inquiring whether anyone would be willing to take us sailing, but everyone shook their heads. One gentleman said he would love to take us, but he had only a very small boat, and his family were coming aboard. He said, 'Son, go onto the dock where the club ferry is, and ask people there.'

I thanked him and went immediately to the dock. The first gentleman I approached, looked at his companions, then at his skipper, a man in his late forties. I explained that I had read many books on sailing, and now wanted to gain practical experience.

'Well,' the skipper said, 'go, call your father and hurry back.' I was airborne with excitement, and raced off to fetch Dad.

Introductions were made aboard the ferry. The skipper was Bill, a Cape Town lawyer. His boat was a 36-foot sloop. He showed me how to hank on a sail and left me to sort out the head sail, which I managed to do correctly. The books Tony had lent me on working as a deckhand were a tremendous help. I understood the terminology, and so learned quickly. I helped slip the mooring and we were off.

Once the sloop was clear of obstructions, we raised the sails and powered under full sail, with a silenced engine.The sloop healed over, picking up speed. We reached out of Simon's Bay, across False Bay, sailing to windward. I helmed, learning to keep the sails full of wind. It was an erratic course but with the wind in my hair and the taste of saltspray on my lips, I fell in love with the sport. I had discovered something in life I wanted to pursue. After that meeting with Bill, eight years passed before I saw him again, getting the opportunity to thank him for giving me my first sailing experience.

The call of the sea was very strong. The next weekend I lugged all my heavy diving gear to the railway station to catch a southbound train along the coast to meet a schoolfriend, Kevin. We wanted to dive for fish. It was not easy using public transport with bulky gear. False Bay is on the Indian Ocean side of the Cape of Good Hope. Cape Town has a warm Mediterranean climate,

Early navigational experience on the Rhine River

with the city built on the slopes of Table Mountain. The area we spearfished had beautiful gullies; beneath the water were

various type of red and yellow coral growing on the rocky reefs.

We loaded our spearguns and began the hunt. Mostly I hunted bream. I never shot at anything that I could not eat. On this particular dive, I missed with every shot taken. The water was reasonably clean and warm. Lying on the surface, I could see the bottom twenty feet below. I dived into a gully, and on surfacing for a breath of air, suddenly saw the most impressive sight in all my years of diving.

First I caught the glimmer of light off fins. As I got closer to the surface, I realised that I was surrounded by a medium-size school of yellowtail. There were about twenty fish, close to my own body length. They were the largest fish I had seen under water. They swam around me, observing me with innocent curiosity. They moved through the water with the elegance of ballerinas. I raised my gun to fire. The fish were close to me and so tightly bunched that aiming was not really necessary.

Then something overcame me. Here I was surrounded by a school of fish that few people would have the opportunity to swim with. They had surrounded me strangely inquisitive, having come in peace. Nature was blessing me with one of its gracious creatures.

What would it be like, I thought, to watch one of those fish wither at the tip of my spear? I lowered my speargun and lay on the surface admiring this marvellous vision. All too soon the yellow tail were gone. I felt proud that I had caused them no harm.

In my class at school, there was a very attractive girl called René who sat three rows behind and was a year older than me. She was the daughter of an outspoken lawyer, and she herself held some strong opinions. As the boycott continued, she spoke harshly about the lack of interest among certain students to continue their studying at home. Our teachers went to great trouble to prepare worksheets so that we could work on our own. René worked hard at whatever she undertook, earning the respect of all the students, even those who criticised her.

I felt more and more drawn to her, although we rarely spoke. Our worlds were different. I loved adventure, especially that which I found in diving and sailing. She loved politics and aspired to become head of the Student Representative Council, a student body elected at school by the pupils.

After six months helping Tony, his boat was finally launched. A month later Tony, his son and two crew began to prepare the boat to sail to the Caribbean. They planned to spend a year cruising around the islands. I wished that I could have joined the crew.

One afternoon my mother sent me to the supermarket across the street from the school. As I was shopping in the aisle, I overheard two gentleman talking about sailing. I lingered within earshot, pretending to be looking for something on the shelves. One man was inquiring about the performance of the other's boat. When they had said goodbye, I walked up to one of them, a middle-aged man, excused myself for eavesdropping, and told him of my interest in sailing, asking if it would be possible to go out with him sometime. He introduced himself as Alex Petersen, a common South African name, but no relation of mine, and told me that he had a 14-foot catamaran on a trailer, which he took out infrequently. He gave me his phone number and told me to ring in a few weeks. When I did, he said that he was extremely busy at work, and did not have the time to sail just then, but that I should keep in touch.

I was not allowed to go to parties, and had no interest in smoking or drinking, but one weekend René was celebrating her fourteenth birthday, and invited the class to a party at her home. This was a party I was not going to miss. My parents did not encourage me to go to parties, but I was allowed to go to this one, being dropped by car at René's home with an agreed time for my mother to call to collect me.

It was a delightful party. René and I danced.

Over the months I was inspired to write poetry about my feelings for René, but I never sent it to her. My shyness prevented me from asking her out, so I fell in love for the first time from afar.

I had a Friday afternoon job in a petshop cleaning the bird cages and fish tanks, and selling animals.Instead of wages, I was given zebra finches and tropical fish. The pet shop belonged to a neighbour. He told me about the Caribbean islands and the tropical jungles of the Amazon delta, from where he imported some of the fish and parrots. I had read about these places and was eager to visit them sometime.

I was allowed to use the phone at the petshop and I used to call René to chat. One day, during a quiet period in the shop, alone but surrounded by the exotic bird calls, I could no longer keep silent about my feelings for her. I picked up the phone several times and dialled her number. Then I would lose my nerve and hang up before the telephone was answered, recomposing myself before dialling again. Eventually I let it ring and she answered it. After some small talk, I blurted out my real purpose, telling René that I was in love with her. In my excited state, I accidentally depressed the cradle and was cut off. By speaking so candidly, I made her feel very uneasy in my company.

René did not return my love. She had a boyfriend whom I knew. Still, I was not sorry that I had confessed my feelings. My boyhood days were over. I had become a teenager in love. It was not an infatuation, because even now, fourteen years later, there is a soft spot in my heart for her. Because René now knew my feelings, school became a different place. René and I were destined never to become friends: I had pushed her away by telling her of my love. Years later, after leaving school, and on the day I launched my yacht, we met again. I had sent her an invitation to the launching. She was a married woman with a young son, I an experienced yachtsman. She had forgiven my foolishness, but the weight of what I had told her in the petshop still left a gulf between us.

I withdrew from my classmates once it was known that I was in love with René and retreated to Lovers' Lane, the quiet roadside part of the playground, in the shade of a large gum tree. Often courting couples met there because it was quiet. At first, watching them, I felt lonely, but I managed to cope with my feelings. I spent most intervals there for the remainder of my high school years.

Many children at school could not help but see me as the son of Mrs Petersen. My mother had taught at Livingstone for nearly 20 years and was feared by troublesome students because she was a tough, no nonsense disciplinarian. Pupils were nervous that if they misbehaved in my presence, I would go home and tell my mother. For this reason

I was not very popular, even though I would not bring home tales.

Those pupils who had heard of my hopes as a diver and sailor, looked at me as if I were crazy. In their eyes, no thirteen-year-old kid should spearfish in shark-infested waters, helm a fishing boat and be interested in yachting. Sailing was only for the rich, so how could this dreamer, the son of a teacher and factory labourer, from a disenfranchised community, be associated with the wealthy class and their yachts? They poked fun at me.

Through hard work, I had saved enough to buy a second-hand wetsuit and I wanted to explore the sea floor with my spear, and also to scuba dive. I spent a weekend away with a diving club at a resort where a local shop was offering a free introductory lesson in scuba diving.

Kevin and I regularly went on diving trips to Cape Point at the tip of the Cape Peninsula. The land near the Point was a nature reserve, where zebra, ostriches and baboons could be seen. The coastal waters around the reserve was not a part of the nature reserve, so hunting underwater was permitted. My mother drove us to the nature reserve, which had become one of our more successful hunting grounds. On one particular dive, we had just caught some aberlone and two crayfish when we sighted a shark. We moved close to each other. It was time to leave the water, and we made it safely to the beach. At no point were we in danger. By understanding who was dominant and who is the intruder, we were able to hunt underwater successfully.

On Saturday afternoons, my mother would drop me at the yacht club in Table Bay harbour. I roamed the dock, asking if anyone needed a crew member. The first two weekends, I walked despondently to the train station in the evening not having been out for a sail. The next weekend I managed to get out on the Sunday. I was told to sit in a particular place and was shifted around from time to time, but I watched and learned the ropes. The following Saturday afternoon I was at the marina again. That day there was a race in the bay. One boat was short of crew. I was welcomed onto the team, and was even given jobs to do during the race. It was a terrific afternoon, even though we came last.

I was becoming a harbour waif, and was easily recognised as the kid who wanted to learn to sail. A committee member, noticed me and one weekend called me into the clubhouse to introduce me to Colin Farlem. Colin had an old 30-foot boat, a wooden and neglected Royal Cape One Design. This boat was really an overgrown dinghy with a cabin. Colin had recently bought it and had no crew.

The boat needed a lot of work to get it in shape. If I was willing to assist with the maintenance, Colin agreed to give me a permanent position on the crew. He kindly offered to teach me what he knew and I sailed with him aboard *Lapwing* for about five years. He was a bachelor in his mid-forties and was always willing to give young people an opportunity to sail. He worked in a bank, was not wealthy, but he had a strong spirit of adventure. He nurtured my sailing, and gave me the opportunity to learn the different tasks on board.

During my second year at high school, I was elected vice-chairman of the History and Pioneering Club. This club organised various lectures given by students, teachers or guest speakers on current affairs; there were also poetry readings and slide presentations on their personal experiences. One guest speaker, an ex-student, spoke and showed his slides on his one-year travels in Antartica as an assistant meteorologist.

I held my position successfully for seven months, yet found it trying to work with René with whom I had to regularly consult because of her position on the Student Representative Council. I did ask her out several times, but she always turned me down. She avoided speaking to me, unless it was a matter to do with the club.

Between 1981 and 1984, I met the round-the-world sailors who used Cape Town as a stopover from Europe to the Indian Ocean, or those coming from Australia, heading west towards South America and the Caribbean. Some arrived in large modern racing yachts — they were participating in the Whitbread around the world race — while others were sailing old wooden boats, some built before 1950. There were the racing sailors, the cruising families, and the men and women who sailed alone. They came mainly from Europe or North America, but there were New Zealanders and Australians too.

These sailors were from all walks of life, but few of them were very rich. Most were either retired, having worked and saved hard or living on board their boats and taking jobs in the ports they called at. They were ordinary people, bonded to the sea and sailing, seeking as simple a lifestyle as they could afford. To join this community, the only prerequisite was that one sailed in a vessel of some kind. I was always welcome aboard their boats, and they helped to fuel my dreams. I wanted a boat on which I could live. Seeing these aqua globetrotters gave me hope.

The people I was really drawn to were the brave single-handed sailors. To my amazement, they were the friendliest and most gregarious of all. At least ten of them came home with me over a five-year period, dined at our table and told us of their adventures.

In 1982, the British Oxygen Corporation sponsored a single-handed around the world race from Newport, Rhode Island. Cape Town was the first stopover before the 17 yachts headed off six weeks later to Sydney, Australia. Then they sailed around Cape Horn to Punta del Este in Uruguay before returning to Newport after covering some 27,000 miles in nine gruelling months.

I was one of the many spectators on the dock to welcome these sailors in. I had read many books about the drive and determination of these lone sailors, but no book could have prepared me for the experience of meeting them. The camaraderie among them was immense.

I too wanted to become a single-hander, and day-dreamed about competing in the BOC race. None of the sailors laughed at me when I expressed this ambition; they encouraged me by inviting me to look over their craft. Many of these sailing giants had begun their racing careers with the single-handed transatlantic race, known as the OSTAR since it had first been sponsored by *The Observer* newspaper. I was told that if I was serious, then that was the race to do.

Colin proposed me for membership of the Royal Cape Yacht Club in 1982. Some members frowned upon a well suntanned sailor becoming a member, but the committee had no problem opening their doors to a fellow yachtsman, irrespective of the colour of his skin. I became much sought-after as a crew member. At sea, no distinction is made between black and white, rich and poor. The sea is a great leveller.

When it became known at the yacht club that I was a diver, I was often asked to snorkel underneath the hulls of members' boats to check on the barnacles and slime. Sailors asked me to recover winch-handles or sunglasses that had been accidentally dropped overboard. I charged ten rand per hour — the equivalent of £4. Soon I had a thriving little business, and this helped to pay for my scuba lessons.

It was a challenge to search for something in the mud some fifteen feet underwater, while holding my breath. I was determined to find any lost items. It meant numerous dives, with lengthy periods in the water. The water in the yacht club basin was dirty. Oil and litter drifted in on the tides from the adjacent commercial harbour. Whenever I came out of the water, my gear was lined with a film of oil. I did not like diving in the harbour, but put up with the discomfort in order to make my dream that much more realisable.

When I had attained my scuba certification, I went more often on scuba dives with new friends. Dad and I snorkelled less frequently, until a day came when I hung up my speargun, never to shoot with it again. I used hired scuba gear, until my mother helped supplement my savings so that I could buy a scuba cylinder and then the diving regulator. After another year, I could afford a buoyancy compensator.

At the yacht club I began scrubbing hulls for a modest fee. Fishing lines and rope had to be freed from propellers, moorings needed checking, more items that had fallen overboard had to be recovered. I saved what I earned, and learnt to appreciate the value of those hard-earned funds.

In December 1984 I left high school. I had done well academically, earning enough grades to get into university, but instead, I chose a career at sea and to study commercial diving at the College of Oceaneering in Los Angles. I had read about the college in a diving magazine. The training was very expensive, but my mother had put aside enough money to enable me to study overseas.

2

THE CALL OF THE SEA

During the race, the water temperature had dropped from four to two degrees, but the fog was as dense as ever. It was cold and miserable on deck; the damp was getting into my bones. Below deck I lit a kerosene lamp to generate some heat and piled on more clothes. My sleeping bag was warm and welcoming.

The twenty-sixth of June 1992 was my nineteenth day out from Plymouth. In the early mornings before breakfast, I would take two or three catnaps, about twenty minutes each. Later in the morning, depending on whether I had things to do on deck, I would take three or four more naps. My afternoon snoozes were an hour long and at night I tried to stay awake. Sometimes the tiredness would not make this possible, so I took a few snatches of sleep every couple of hours. At first I used an alarm clock to wake me, but as I grew used to sleeping intermittently my body clock took over.

My nineteenth day was like any other day, except that I could not sleep in the afternoon. Conditions had deteriorated. The fog was a blanket of fine water droplets and, in the breeze, the air temperature felt as if it was below zero. I tried to stay below, but felt uneasy and kept being drawn out on the deck.

It was soon clear that the fog had become patchy. It showed signs of clearing. Hundreds of birds, mostly terns with a few gannets, circled the boat, taking flight as my bow sliced towards them, under spinnaker at more than ten knots. The sun broke through the layers of fog. I felt exhilarated. Overhead I heard the sonic boom of an aircraft flying beyond the speed of sound, a daily intrusion on the peaceful surroundings.

The *Stella-r* crossed the continental shelf onto the Grand Banks. When I came into the shallower waters, my Stowe electronic depth sounder began showing a reading of 150 meters. According to the instrument, the water was another degree colder, near freezing. The seas were significantly larger as we surfed with a following sea and wind. No longer was I in the warm Gulf Stream; now it was the icy Labrador current. I had expected to see fishing vessels, but nothing was visible in the fog. The Grand Banks had been overfished, and few fishermen could earn a living there.

Suddenly the fog cleared, so I went back on deck to trim the spinnaker. Less than a mile away was a giant iceberg and I was sailing directly towards it! The gap was closing rapidly. Seven-eighths of an iceberg is below the water. I half-expected to hear the crunching sound of my hull running aground as I tried to steer the boat to the iceberg's lee. The spinnaker collapsed and began to flap violently in the breeze. It was time to take it down before it started to tear.

I charged onto the foredeck to pull down on a rope that controlled a sock-like cover in which the spinnaker was stowed when it was not in use. This cover resembled the outer skin of a sausage (the spinnaker being the meat). The entire sausage was hoisted to the top of the mast. When all the control lines of the spinnaker had been set, the sock would be hoisted to the top of the spinnaker and the line secured to a cleat, its contents having been released. The spinnaker was then trimmed. When the sail was being doused, the sock was just pulled down and the reverse took place. The process took only a few seconds after the 'sausage' was hoisted to the masthead, but dousing the sail while sailing fast towards the iceberg was a frenzied job.

I rushed back to the cockpit to gybe the main sail; this means that I moved the sail from one side of the boat to the other while sailing downwind, and then steered away. The visibility was deteriorating once more, but I managed to stay clear of the iceberg. I continued to sail downwind of it, but a lot more slowly. Soon I would need to gybe back onto my previous course and return my attention to the race. My attention was focused on deck as I took in the main sheet. Suddenly I felt and heard a thud. The boat slowed down for a minute or two, then continued as normal but with a lump of ice drifting in its wake. I had hit what Canadians call a growler, a very small iceberg about the size of a family car. The boat gybed. I rushed below to assess the damage, but found none, although it had seemed a hard enough thud.

I had been fortunate. Perhaps a spirit was looking after me. Had I slept my normal routine, I would probably have hit the main iceberg and sunk. In those cold waters, one could not survive for more than two or three days on a life raft before succumbing to hypothermia.

My memories of Table Mountain and my teenage years were like a candle in a dark room, and helped me cope. Later in the day my confidence was restored. I did not rehoist the spinnaker until the next morning, and sailed with a headsail poled out to one side. No one around could give me comfort. My fellow competitors were out of radio range.

**

My thoughts turned to the country I was sailing towards. The first time I had thought of America was as a schoolboy dreaming of attending the College of Oceaneering in Los Angeles. It was the best college in the world in which to study commercial diving, according to a survey taken among the nine largest diving companies and published in a diving magazine.

I had arrived in los Angeles at age seventeen, innocent and knowing nobody in the city. On my third day I became really homesick. I set out in search of a marina, looking for a friendly face, met a man of about sixty-five who invited

32

me onto his boat for coffee. Arnold Cook was fascinated that my parents would allow me to fend for myself in a foreign country. He understood the freedom they had given me, appreciating the strength it had taken to untie the apron strings.

Over steaming coffee, I learnt that Arnold had terminal cancer and was too weak to do manual work. He reminisced about his days on the Pacific where he had spent two decades as a naval officer. Separated from his wife for several years, he had decided to live on board the 43-foot *Chantey Dragon*. His spirit of adventure was unaffected by his illness and he soon made me forget my homesickness.

At the end of the afternoon, Arnold drove me back to my youth hostel in Harbour City, a suburb of Los Angeles. As I was getting out of the car, he asked me where I would be staying after my few days at the hostel. I had not given it any thought. Arnold offered me a cabin on board the *Chantey Dragon*, in exchange for which I could help him with repair jobs on the boat.

The year at the College of Oceaneering was exciting. Twenty-three students, starry-eyed with hope, began the course with me. I took two courses. The first was on air diving. We studied the theory of diving and decompression. Decompression is the release of an inert gas, in this case nitrogen, which is built up within the body under pressure while diving. As a diver comes back to the surface after being underwater, the rate of ascent needs to be controlled to prevent what is called the bends, a painful occurrence, mostly in the joints, when the ascent is too rapid. We spent the first few dives in a large tank of water, becoming familiar with the gear, then progressed into the murky waters of the harbour where we performed simple tasks underwater and gained experience of looking after the person in the water. The course, which lasted for three months, was hard. Some students discovered that they were not cut out for diving. The numbers began to dwindle.

At the end of the third month, there were just eleven of us left.

The second course, non-destructive testing, lasted for four months and involved learning to use magnetic particle inspection set up by electric currents, to find hairline cracks in metals under water. We also studied ultrasonic testing to discover metallic failure before it showed up on the metal's surface.

When I was not diving, I was sailing. Since I lived in a marina, I met many people. At weekends I was frequently in demand to crew for the racing teams. I began crewing regularly on a 35-foot racing boat, often training during week nights, and other times sailed with an aircraft engineer who had a 22-foot boat. As my final exams approached, those luxurious evening sails had to stop.

As Arnold's health was deteriorating, we put to sea less frequently, and I would often come in to find him doubled over with pain. The doctors said they could do nothing for him while he was on the boat, but he refused to budge. As long as he could manage on board, he would stay. He was content to stay in his bunk or sit in a deck chair. I was afraid that I would come back one day and find him dead.

One afternoon I walked in and Arnold said: 'I have a message for you from Teresa Piccard.'

I was stunned. During my last months in South Africa, I had worked on a luxury 65-foot French yacht, owned by a French oil magnate who had bought it for his daughter. She was three years older than me and had a warm smile. I had spent hours scrubbing the deck of the yacht and she deliberately walked over it with dirty shoes. Despite her good looks, I thought she was a brat. The next weekend she ordered me to fetch some parcels from her car. I was not a hired hand, and had merely been helping out in exchange for some sailing in the bay.

' "Thank you" is such a small phrase and doesn't take much,' I said as she was walking away.

Some days later, I was sitting alone in the yacht club reading. I heard Teresa's French accent behind me, offering me a drink. I declined, but I was dazed by her physical beauty. Shyly, I went back to my magazine, unsuccessfully trying to ignore her presence.

'For a boy who tries to teach me manners, you should have a few of your own,' she said, sitting down next to me, uninvited.

'I am not a whelp who orders people around and stomps over their hard work,' I replied, walking off to another table.

We were the only two people in the lounge.

'Come back here,' she sighed.

I detected a hint of sadness in her voice.

'Miss Piccard,' I said, 'inside the bar are many men who would love to drink with you.'

I felt that I had nothing in common with this heiress, an only child. I tried to read, but could not concentrate. Her presence was too strong and I kept stealing glances at her.

Eventually Teresa walked over to me and asked, smiling warmly, 'Neal, may I join you, please?'

I was dumbstruck.I motioned her to a chair and put down my magazine.

'Truce?' she asked. 'Join me for dinner.'

'Only if you allow me to take *you* to dinner.'

'Okay, where and when?'

'I have no car. You can meet me outside the train station, Friday evening at six o'clock.'

With that I left. I had no intention of taking her to a restaurant. She had dined at the finest tables around the world, but I could not afford to entertain her lavishly. I wanted to see Teresa again, but it had to be somewhere I could afford.

On the appropriate evening we met.

35

'What's that?' she said, pointing to the wicker basket in my hand.

'A surprise.'

We set off to the bus station, Teresa asking me every so often where we were going. We boarded a bus for the lovely seaside residential area on the slopes of Table Mountain, five miles south of the city. Teresa looked at me strangely. In all her visits to Cape Town, she had never taken public transport. She lived several months of the year in Monte Carlo, but had spent three summers living in an elite suburb on the eastern slopes of Table Mountain. Her father had bought a mansion and kept two people employed full-time tending to the house and huge gardens. We got off the bus on the lower slopes of Table Mountain and walked to the cableway station. She smiled when she realised that I was taking her to the top of Table Mountain, away from the noise of the city.

When we reached the summit, I found a secluded rocky outcrop and opened the wicker basket. I took out a red rose and, without a word, gave it to her. Terry blushed. She had expected me to bring her to a fancy restaurant that took American Express cards. Instead, before her lay a vista that she had never seen before. We could look over the bay, the sun setting in the west and the first of the street lights coming on, illuminating the warm night.

Then I spread out a tablecloth and served my simple meal of lettuce, tomato and avocado pear salad from our garden, cold meats, fresh bread and cheese. Teresa loved it.

I opened a bottle of sparkling wine. We chatted as we sipped and ate. Teresa was an only child. Her mother had died a long time before and she had no memories of her. Nannies had raised and educated her. Her father travelled extensively, building his oil empire, and rarely had time to spend with his daughter. When Teresa was nine, she was sent to boarding school and then, eight years later, to college in England, but she had dropped out within a year.

The young millionairess did no work and enjoyed parties immensely, having had little time for lectures. Anything she wanted, her father gave her, from credit cards to apartments to expensive cars.

Slowly everything grew quiet as darkness came, except for the birds. There was not a breath of wind to rustle the leaves, nor a cloud in the brilliantly coloured sky. A ship was coming into Table Bay. Then the new moon rose in the east, the southern hemisphere stars filled the skies.

This view was a perfection Terry's money could never buy. I felt sorry for her, knowing that one day she would inherit many millions of dollars, and yet be lonely, a prisoner in her privileged world. Her father's money could not buy her happiness. I put my arm around her shoulders. She snuggled up quietly. Then we kissed. I felt like a king, her protector.

I did not tell Terry that I was going abroad to college in a matter of two months, feeling that we were passing through each other's lives. We never spoke about tomorrow, for she and I had no tomorrow in South Africa. We met none of each other's friends, because they would not approve of us seeing each other, though in the yacht club we had mutual associates with whom we went sailing. In time, I thought, she would get bored with our quiet relationship, but she never got that opportunity. I left Cape Town without saying goodbye.

Terry flew over once she had tracked me down in Los Angeles and contacted me, but I knew that our romance was over. I really liked her, but we came from such different worlds and that would present insuperable difficulties.

I went to see her and spent several hours talking about how we felt about each other. She was angry at my sudden departure.

When I returned to the boat later that evening, Arnold was not there. I phoned his ex-wife, who told me that he had rung her to say that he was dying. She had sent an ambulance to take him to hospital. I went to see him the next day. He was weak, but cheerful.

'Look after my boat,' he said faintly, 'and yourself.'

At the end of March 1985, I took my final exams of the diving course. Hours after the last paper we heard that ten of the eleven of us had made it.

We had a wild graduation party. Somewhere in the crowd I had lost Terry. I went looking for her. I found her among a few strangers, sitting on someone's lap getting her thigh stroked and smoking dope. I felt jealous and angry. I yanked her up onto her feet, but she slapped me in the face. It was a shock to see Terry taking drugs and acting violently.

The following morning, Terry came down to the boat. She was her normal self and acted as if nothing had happened. I was too disgusted to say anything and decided to walk away.

As I was leaving, Terry tossed me a set of keys.

'I bought you a car,' she said smiling.

I put the keys down and walked off without saying a word. At the head of the dock, parked besides Terry's black Ferrari, was a red Porsche convertible, my favourite sports car. I walked past. This was not the world in which I had grown up and I wanted no part of it. I had earned the things I wanted, working hard for them. No one was going to buy my respect.

After my exams, I took a holiday in Sausalito, Northern California, while Terry returned to Monte Carlo to visit her father.

Sailing in San Francisco Bay, I learnt an all-important lesson about the sea. Late one morning, I borrowed a sailing dinghy and took it out into the bay. Suddenly a stiff breeze freshened, driving me off course and towards the Golden Gate Bridge. It was exhilarating sailing — I had never been in a dinghy before — but near the bridge the craft capsized.

I put on my life jacket and tried everything I knew to bring the boat upright, to no avail. The tide was ebbing and carrying me towards the bridge and the open sea. I thought about abandoning the dingy and swimming for shore. Then I considered trying to make it to a houseboat, about half-a-mile away, to summon help, but the three nearest houseboats looked deserted.

It was getting cold in the water, and I started to shiver. No one would miss me until well after sundown, several hours away. Some yachts sailed by less than two hundred metres away. I tried to hail them, but it was hopeless. My shivering now was becoming uncontrollable. Parts of the dinghy began drifting off — first the centre board, then the rudder — but I was too frozen to leave the capsized hull. My whole being concentrated on staying with the boat, because together we would be easier to find. I tied a rope around my waist. If I lost my strength, at least the life jacket would keep me afloat and the rope would not let me drift too far away from the boat.

I do not know how long I was in the water before a power boat sailor spotted my capsized hull and came over to investigate. He had been out for a leisurely afternoon's fishing. When he came alongside, he saw me hanging onto the dinghy. I was too cold to wave, but I had known that he had seen the hull. He helped me into his boat and I told him about the gear drifting off. We recovered it all.

Shortly after, the fog began rolling in. With my sail down, the power boat sailor, who had not even told me his name, was able to tow the dinghy upright back to Sausalito. He took off his woollen jumper and insisted that I put it on.

Once back safely on shore, I returned his jumper and asked how much I owed him for his fuel and time. He would hear nothing of it, but I said that I would like to repay him in some way for saving my life.

'Son, one day you will help someone at sea,' he said softly. 'That will be repayment enough to me.'

His words have remained with me and I took a vow always to help someone in distress.

My eighteenth birthday passed quietly with a few close friends in the marina. Terry returned from Monte Carlo, but she had become a stranger.

In a matter of months in California, Terry had become a drug addict. I rarely saw her sober. She was either high or deeply depressed. I tried to take her sailing, where she could not get her hands on any drugs, but her withdrawals were so severe that it was impossible to handle her. She kept telling me that if I loved her, I would let her be happy. I begged her to get help, but she never did. Instead, she left me and I never saw her again. A year later, at twenty-one years old, Terry was dead. She was under the influence of drugs when she lost control of her light aircraft and crashed into a mountain slope in Brazil.

Back in South Africa, my maternal grandmother had died at the age of 86. I felt guilty that she had passed away while I was fulfilling my dreams, and that she had never really understood why the sea was more important to me than a university degree. She had wanted me to go to university to study law, but I could not bear the thought of more studies and a law career, when my desire was to dive.

My mother surprised me by coming to Los Angeles for a holiday. She stayed aboard the *Chantey Dragon*, using it as a base from which to travel alone around California. She visited San Francisco for a few days, then returned to Los Angeles with a young British woman she had met who was also on holiday. Together they visited Universal Studios, Pasadena Botanical Gardens and the planetarium, and one weekend I took them to Disneyland. My mother sailed with me to Santa Catalina Island, 25 miles from the harbour, where we spent a night camping on a beach. For the Fourth of July celebrations, we travelled to Arizona for three days to walk around the rim of the Grand Canyon.

It was delightful to have my mother with me. The boat felt homely again. Often she visited Arnold in hospital with me. She cooked my favourite dishes for me, and sometimes we ate out.

When she left, I travelled north to the Canadian border, but I was not allowed across until I had obtained a Canadian visa. I was told to apply for one at the Canadian consulate in Seattle. Unfortunately the consulate wanted to see my student documents, which I had left in California, before they could issue me with a visa. This was to be the beginning of many frustrating dealings with bureaucracy. How could a government official deny me the right to cross land on our planet? In my own country, I had been denied fundamental human rights because of the colour of my skin. Now I was denied the rights of admission to another country because I lacked a piece of paper!

Instead, I bought a bus ticket to Yosemite National Park. It was early August when I arrived in the park with my backpack and small tent. I wanted to walk among the glaciers and climb the mountains, where I spent two months preparing myself mentally for the isolation that I would face one day at sea. I walked to the summit of three steep peaks, carrying a few supplies and water. The paths were not difficult, but I had not got used to the altitude. I had to discipline myself to walk slowly, and take more rests. I chose little-used routes. Once off the main paths, I did not meet anyone for several days. I shared the mountains with the brown bear and the coyote.

These experiences proved to be invaluable. I had found peace within myself and nature. The isolation helped me learn to like myself, and accept my short-comings.

A month after I came down from the mountain, I decided that it was time to return to South Africa. I wanted to see my parents.

I flew to New York for two days. On the same day that my flight from New York took off, carrying me to London, Arnold died peacefully in his hospital bed. Several months later I received a letter from his wife telling me of his death and saying that the *Chantey Dragon* had been sold.

**

In mid-ocean eight years later, I thought about Arnold Cook. My dream had been to own a vessel, and here I was, having realised that dream. Was Arnold able to glimpse into my future and did this prompt him to help me? I will never know, but it was my nine months at college that had enabled me to become a professional sailor.

3

A CAREER AT SEA

The collision with the ice-island had shaken me. I stayed on deck for the rest of the day. The fog closed in again and remained dense for another three days. Eventually I got my nerve back, and was able to obtain some sleep.

The following morning I discovered that the boat had been damaged and was taking in water through the hull in the forward section. Fortunately, there was a watertight bulkhead and the leak could be contained. There was a crack on the hull but I could not see it. Looking over the bow, I was tempted to put on a wetsuit and dive over the side to determine the full extent of the damage, but the sea was too choppy.

I had put up the genoa after the collision. In the morning I replaced it with the spinnaker and set a course for St John's, Newfoundland. This was on my route, following the great circle. A great circle route is an imaginary line that is the shortest distance on a curved surface between two places. My plan was to sail close to the coast in the shallow water where I would be less likely to hit an iceberg. If the leak in the hull got worse, I would be close enough to land to put into a port.

By going close to shore I could use the coastal radio to make a few phone calls. This would lift my morale. I had spent so many years dreaming about this race and making sacrifices to sail in it, that one way or another I was determined to finish.

***

In late 1985 I had returned to South Africa equipped with a little knowledge and some experience of commercial diving. It was my dream to build a yacht through saving some of the income I had earned by diving. I visited diving companies around Cape Town in search of work; they serviced and maintained platforms in the gas fields off the south-eastern South African coast. I was told that I needed a Department of Manpower certificate. My American qualifications in commercial diving were not recognised in South Africa, yet these firms were hiring British and American divers who had the same qualifications as myself.

I went to the Department of Manpower, and was told that I would have to retrain at the local diving school in Simonstown, even though, as a sport diver, I had learnt what this school taught. However, I did discover that I could get work diamond-diving. I still needed a Manpower certificate, but I could get a temporary exemption from the Department of Mining.

There was a shortage of divers in Port Nolloth, a small town on the north-western coast of South Africa, close to the Namibian border. The Cape Town office of one large group interviewed and hired me, and also handled the Department of Mines permission request.

In January 1986, I travelled to Port Nolloth with Andy Kean, a fellow diver who had worked for the company for a year. Andy lived in the empty company house, and gave me a bed for the night.

In the morning I went to see the personnel department. I met the hard-core Afrikaaner general manager. He asked me to sign a one-year contract. No one had told me about this, and I did not feel easy about committing myself to a full year with the company.

Then I was sent over to the diving supervisor who explained my duties. I was to help the other divers get into their gear, and after their dive, help them undress. On deck while a diver was in the water, I was to ensure that he had enough air hose, and on his return, I had to retrieve the air hose. Underwater I was to move the huge suction hose

44

into the gravel to suck it up, removing cobbles that were too large to pass up the mining hose. The supervisor's advice was to work hard and I would earn good money. I discussed the contract with him, and he told me that if I wanted the job, I would have to sign it.

So I went back to the general manager, gave him the signed contract and asked about accommodation. He told me that I would have to find my own. The company provided accommodation only for single white divers. This was my first encounter with racialism as a working person, and the start of my determination to overcome it.

South Africa was and still is a racist country. The law books stated categorically that black people were inferior, and should be treated as such. Since the colonising of South Africa by the Dutch in the sixteenth century, children have been raised to believe in black inferiority and white supremacy. *Apartheid* is a codified system of racial segregation.

My childhood had been sheltered, but now I felt great rage at being told where I could and could not stay. I left the office and went out to a public coin box. I called the president of the company and asked him to tell me why I was not being allowed to stay in the company house. He said that this was South Africa, not California, and put down the phone. Soon afterwards I was tracked down and summoned to the general manager's office. He made it clear that if I did not like things as they were, I could resign, but he reminded me of my contract. He then said that he had found me a room, gave me the address and dismissed me.

The room in the house overlooked the harbour. My career as a diamond diver had begun. I loved the quiet of the sea floor, and found that for most of the day I could be left undisturbed with my own thoughts. We worked between ten and fourteen hours a day, seven days a week, weather permitting. When the seas were rough, we had time off. I spent those hours studying for the Department of

Manpower exams which I hoped to take in September. Unfortunately my application was refused because I did not have sufficient training. I was annoyed because the college where I had trained in California was regarded as one of the world's finest.

In Port Nolloth I became aware of pervasive racial prejudice. On days that we did not go to sea, we provided meals for ourselves. One evening I felt like eating out with Andy Kean, who had become one of my closest friends, and four other divers. We decided to go to the only restaurant in town. We walked in and sat down. Within minutes the manager came over, telling the white-skinned divers that they knew they could not bring a 'coloured' into his restaurant. He asked me to leave. The humiliation and anger I felt was immense. My colleagues, including Andy, just shrugged their shoulders as I got up, and continued to order as if nothing had happened.

I did the same job as the other divers, earned the same wages and was a respectable human being, but I was being denied my human rights because of the colour of my skin. It was not the last time I was to be refused service in that racist town.

At sea I had to work with bigots. They obviously found it hard to be tolerant to me, but I gave them no opportunity to fault my work. I began to understand their make-up. Inside, they were deeply suspicious and even afraid of people who were different from them. I was the first educated black person many of them had met, and I had studied at an overseas college, an opportunity their wealth had not afforded them.

The black deckhands on the boats swallowed hard and spent their life accepting the widespread prejudice. They did not like to be segregated, but did not have the energy to fight it. Black graduates of the diving school in Simonstown, were treated like the deckhands.

I had difficulty communicating with the people of my own racial group because of the language barrier. My knowledge of Afrikaans, the language predominantly spoke in the rural districts of South Africa, was very weak. I think of it as the language of my oppressors. Afrikaans and English are the two official languages in South Africa. I felt that when I speak it to a racist, I was lowering myself to his level, yet I did try to learn Afrikaans.

I lived for the day when I would sail into Port Nolloth in my own yacht. Every day on that coast was like living in hell.

I felt lonely, especially because I was shuffled from boat to boat, each lead diver sad to let me go. I got on well with most of my workmates, even making a few friends. My reputation as a hard worker grew. Several people noticed my determination to succeed. Some encouraged me; others grew jealous.

Before long, the job became monotonous. Each working day I did two dives. I moved gravel through the suction hose to the surface and left rock piles on the sea floor. The alluvial diamonds are found in the gravel. Since the specific gravity of a diamond is higher than the gravel, the diamonds are found on the bedrock.

Visibility on the seabed was atrocious. The second dive was shorter because residual nitrogen was still in the bloodstream after the first dive, making the non-decompression less. I detested getting into a wet diving suit, but I had to make the most of it.

To earn a living at sea is not easy. The most valuable lesson *I* learnt about the sea was that, irrespective of a man's colour or wealth, in the eyes of God all men are equal. Aboard those diamond boats, we were all dependent on one another for our survival. Skin colour did not matter.

I wrote a letter to a friend from high school, with whom I had shared my ambitions:

I hate this town. In one's time off there is nothing to do. Tonight I walked to the beach and sat on the rocks staring out to sea. It was a beautiful sunset. I was thinking and dreaming about some day in the future when my yacht will be bobbing at anchor off this beach. Maybe I will not have to work so hard any more and will appreciate what I have when I remember the days like now, days when I struggled so hard. I will continue to seek my fortunes, though I wish there was no contract restricting me.

After three months in Port Nolloth, the family from whom I rented, needed my room. The harbourmaster told me about a vacant house that was up for sale in the white part of town. After contacting the owners, it was agreed that I could stay, rent free, provided I showed the house to prospective buyers and kept vandals away. To legally stay in that section of town, I could not live in the main house. I moved into the servants' quarters but had keys to the house where I could use the shower and bath.

When it was known that I could let prospective buyers see the house, I got several visitors, mostly in the evening. One afternoon, an Afrikaner of about fifty years old came around. He was very impolite. I let him in and then left him alone to look around. After a brief tour, he demanded to see the servants' quarters. When I told the harbourmaster about this man, he asked me to describe him. He recognised him as the mayor of the town, who had been the last tenant in the house. He was furious. This man had come to see where I was living, because it was in a part of town where people of my racial background were not welcome. Two days later my electricity was disconnected.

Fortunately, the sea grew rough for several days and I was able to go home to Cape Town. Often when I had phoned my parents, I was close to tears with anger and frustration. If it had not been for the contract I had signed, I would have left my job. Back home, I was able to vent my anger. My mother understood my resentment at the prejudice I was encountering. She had had similar experiences. Her gentle advice was to swallow hard and be strong.

My return to the diamond coast was not an easy journey. Shortly after arriving back, the head of the company announced new financial terms on the cartage bonus; the dive team would have to take a large pay cut. I saw this as my chance to leave. The contract that was binding me to that miserable town could now be broken because the company was reducing our agreed commission rate. The company saw my argument, and paid me off.

I spent some weeks in Cape Town, fruitlessly trying to find work in the oil fields and harbours, but then I went back to the Department of Manpower to tell them of my training and experience, and was allowed to sit their exams the following September.

I called a few companies on the diamond coast to find a temporary job with good commission. A small company in Hondeklip Bay, eighty miles south of Port Nolloth, needed divers badly to assemble a diving system. They offered me work and accommodation. My home was in the so-called white side of town.

The company worked two boats twenty miles to the south in a bay surrounded by red cliffs. It was rumoured that diamonds as large as thumbnails could be picked out of the cliff face. The work was very hard and treacherous because the company did not observe the necessary safety standards. The divers were not well-trained and often took risks. One diver was killed when he became trapped by a large rock and lost his air supply.

After I had helped to get the vessels working, the company rewarded me by removing me from it's house. I was told that the town's mayor and aldermen had objected to the presence of a black person in 'their' section of town. The company claimed that it had too much to lose to fight this injustice, yet I was not compensated for the humiliation and hurt. Instead, I was given a shack on the coast some distance from the town, with no fresh water, no toilet, and no cooking facilities. A mattress was left on a gravel floor to sleep on.

I was permitted to go to the company house, where the other divers lived, only in dire emergencies. It was expected of me to wash in the sea and find a place among the rocks to use as a toilet.

Swallowing very hard, I moved into the shack. The job was needed if my dream to own a yacht was to come true. Yet anger was building up inside me like an active volcano that had been corked to prevent it from erupting. I asked for a pay rise, but this was denied. My responsibilities as lead diver increased unofficially to supervising the diving operation, but I worked under a puppet supervisor who received credit for a job well done and was paid more than me.

Soon Dawn Diamonds, an offshore diving company specialising in deep water exploration, learnt that I was interested in leaving inshore diving. On a visit to Cape Town, I was offered a job, provided I qualified. This gave me an incentive to return to Hondeklip Bay, and to use my free time to study.

At the end of September 1986 I sat the Department of Manpower exam. It was a snip. The standard was lower than my training at the College of Oceaneering. After the exam, I returned to Hondeklip Bay for the last time to wait for my results. My shack was as forlorn and un-welcoming as ever; life in the town was wretched. On days when it was too rough to dive, I sat on the rocks watching the seas pounding in, tossing up spray. It was a lonely existence, not being able to visit my friends in the company house.

Then the results came. A brown government envelope was delivered to the office. In view of the office, I opened it and read that I had passed. Looking out at the diamond boats riding at their moorings, I realised that never again would I have to go to sea in them, I walked back to the office, showed the letter to the general manager and resigned.

Now I could accept an offer from Dawn Diamonds, offshore on the *Trident Cape*, their mother ship. Dawn

Diamonds organised a lift for me from Hondeklip Bay to Port Nolloth. A chartered fishing boat took us and fresh food out to the *Trident Cape*, some thirty nautical miles to the south of the town. She was about 400 feet long and painted a bright orange. Before being used on the diamond coast, she had been a support ship in the Singapore oil fields.

I was shown to my cabin which I shared with another diver, and was given a brief tour. It appeared to be a happy ship, reasonably clean, with plenty to eat. Our tour of duty would be twenty-eight days, after which there were two weeks shore leave in Cape Town. The salary was good, though our commission on the diamonds we brought up was poor.

At seven the following morning, I reported to the dive station on the ship's bow. The latest diving technology enabled us to speak to one another underwater. We had first-class safety measures and travelled to the seafloor in a cage lowered or raised by winch, containing emergency breathing equipment. Our air was fed down an umbilical, a 300-foot collection of tubes carrying two air supplies, a communications cable and a hotwater pipe for pumping warm water into the diving suits.

The dive team in the water which comprised of two or three divers was working at 120 feet and spent just over an hour on the seabed. At the end of the shift, we followed our umbilical back to the cage, and were brought to the surface at a controlled speed. At thirty feet we stopped for a few minutes for in-water decompression, before coming back on deck. Two tenders were designated to help each diver remove his gear.

Once stripped to our bathing suits, we entered a large deck chamber and were recompressed to forty feet, breathing pure oxygen all the way down. The divers transferred to the main part of the chamber where there were mattresses and blankets. We stretched out and for intervals of twenty minutes breathed oxygen from a face mask. When not breathing oxygen, we took breaks of five minutes to breathe the air.

Exhausted from our dive, we sat back, but were not allowed to sleep. Sitting in the chamber was the only time in the working day when we could relax and maybe read. Holding a conversation while breathing oxygen was impossible. We stayed in the chamber until the decompression schedule which lasted almost two hours, was over.

Mining diamonds on the sea bed.
Photographer: Neal Petersen

The dive team placed their lives in the hands of their fellow divers. During the dive someone on deck ran the control panel for the divers in the water. Depth gauges and time were monitored to calculate decompression schedules as the panel operator communicated with the divers, carrying out their requests and controlling their ascent and the decompression in the water. Once the divers were on deck, responsibility was handed over to the chamber operator. Often we rotated jobs, with the panel operator running the chamber for the same dive team.

Whoever drove the chamber was responsible for maintaining depth, for timing the periods spent at depth on oxygen and air, and for catering to the divers' needs. When the team was in the main chamber, coffee or tea would be sent down in a separate pressurised compartment.

My diary entry for 28 November 1986 reads:

We have been diving non-stop now for the last ten days. Finding few diamonds. Working in 150 feet of water. Short bottom times and long times in the chamber. Weather has been absolutely fabulous. Seas are calm, little breeze and warm.

Should have left two weeks ago, but the team is a diver short. I volunteered to stay, not minding the time offshore at all. The longer I remain here, the more I can save.

Several times in the course of my time as a diver on the west coast, I asked myself why I was risking so much for so little. The answer was always the same: so that one day I could have my boat and sail the oceans of the world.

Three days after my diary entry, I was on two weeks' shore leave, my first trip to Cape Town since I had passed my diving exams. I had been on the *Trident Cape* for forty-two days. The drive home in the company mini-bus felt like eternity.

My leave was spent in the library hunting for books on sailing, and at the yacht club with my few sailing friends, but I did not have a chance to go sailing or to go to the beach. All too suddenly it was over and I was back on the *Trident Cape*. We had a new captain aboard, a Scottish tanker man, Ian Wingate, soft-spoken and polite, but commanding authority.

At Christmas I went on shore leave again. Cape Town was hot and busy. Dad was working and I rarely saw him. I spent time with my mother, telling her at length of my yearning for a boat. She was sceptical, but did not discourage me, just made me aware of my financial limitations. My diving was earning me a fair income, but it was not enough for a boat. Bank loans were not easily come by and the interest on them was prohibitively high.

Still, on that shore leave I visited a few yacht brokers who sold second-hand yachts. My older sister Jan was home from Johannesburg for the holidays. On New Year's Day we went sailing on a boat belonging to a close friend of mine, DeWett Schonken, a liberal Afrikaner. I had met him when I had hung around the marina as a kid. In those days he had a thirty-foot boat, but he was building a new one. DeWett wanted to sail to the Caribbean and had asked Jan and me to join him when his new boat was complete. I was tempted.

Back on the *Trident Cape*, I heard from the Health and Safety Executive, a body that regulates diving in the North Sea oil fields, granting me permission to take their exams. I contacted the diving school in Plymouth, England and arranged to do the exams in mid-May. Then I told my supervisor of my decision to leave the Diamond Coast. He not only encouraged me to pursue my ambitions, but told me that there would always be a job for me.

By April 1986, I had saved enough money to do the exam. I left the ship and my fellow divers. I flew to London, and then took a train to Plymouth. Fort Bovisand, where the exam was held, was a fortress guarding the entrance to Plymouth Sound. It had been converted into a diving school with a small craft harbour. I had read about the school three years before when I was researching information on diving courses.

From the fort, on clear evenings, I could see the Eddystone Lighthouse seven miles away. This was one of the landmarks of the transatlantic race that I had read about. I visited the marina where the boats would assemble. The next race was thirteen months away.

A large multi-hull series was being sailed. I strolled down the dock, admiring the trimarans and I took a vow to have my own boat in the 1988 race.

I was the only person to take the two-day theoretical exam and passed. Then I headed north for Aberdeen where I had to do a five-day offshore survival programme, and immediately afterwards I began looking for a diving job in the North Sea. I knocked on many doors without luck. Those divers who had jobs offshore were hanging onto them.

I was despondent. My savings were fast disappearing, but I found work in a Bengalese restaurant in Aberdeen washing dishes until three in the morning. This meant that I could look for work during the day.

One day I was given the name of a former diving superintendent on the west coast of Scotland. I rang Tom McKlusky and he offered me a job diving for scallops. I packed my bags and headed for Glasgow.

Tom was a tall weedy man in his mid forties with a full beard. He came from near Glasgow, but had spent much of his life working in the North Sea and the Persian Gulf. When the recession hit the oil industry, Tom formed his own diving company to do harbour work such as building new breakwaters. All went well until one harbour authority failed to pay him. After a legal wrangle, he closed down the company, taking his small compensation and buying a boat for scallop fishing. We used scuba gear to swim along the seabed in water depths ranging from 30 to 50 feet, picking up scallops.

We spent several weeks diving the island of Arran in the Firth of Clyde. At first my catch was limited, but slowly it improved. I was earning a living, and enjoying myself. We dived every day we could. When Tom was in the water, I was running the boat. It was a hard but healthy life and Tom taught me a lot about seamanship. Once a week we sailed in to a small seaside town to sell our catch.

When the large scallops were hard to find, we ventured to the Isle of Gigha, around the Mull of Kintyre, sixty miles from the Clyde. The scallops were plentiful and the locals friendly. Often we dived in strong tides. It got so bad that we could work only on the slack tides. We sold our catch in West Loch Tarbet, twenty miles east.

One day on our return, we were called on the radio by a local fishing boat which had got a line in its propeller. I dived to free it. In the evening, after they had a full day at sea, they came over with a few lobsters for our dinner.

Tom and I decided to return to Arran to try a different fishing ground. We were able to keep our heads above water financially. Because I lived on board, I could save most of my earnings.

One night the winds were very fresh. We dragged our anchor and resettled in a more sheltered bay. At dawn the winds continued to freshen. It was near a gale force 10, so there would be no diving. Mid-morning, Tom left the cosy fo'c'sle for the wheelhouse to fetch his pipe. The VHF radio was on and he overheard a conversation between a lifeboat and another vessel.

Tom summoned me to the wheelhouse. The conversation was with a yacht, which was up on the rocks. The lifeboat was trying to pull her off, to no avail in the high winds. We called up the lifeboat to find out their exact location, weighed anchor and ten minutes later were standing off the two vessels. The yacht was a chartered 38-footer. She was up a little way on the rocks, with the tide falling. An inflatable lifeboat with outboard engines was struggling to tow her off, but it did not have enough power.

We volunteered our help, but the lifeboat did not look kindly on our offer. There were six seaman in the inflatable, and four people on the yacht, so no one could be taken off the yacht. We watched this midget-sized vessel attempting to drag the monster off the rocks. We got fed up watching them achieve nothing. With a fast-falling tide, the job would soon become more difficult.

I raised the yacht on the radio and told them that Tom and I were yachtsmen and that our vessel was capable of towing them to safety. The lifeboat cut in to say that this was their business, and that we should stay out of the way. I told the skipper that we would return to our anchorage, but if they wanted our help, they should call. With that, I spun the wheel hard over and opened power towards our anchorage.

Minutes later the yacht's skipper radioed us, requesting our help. We went back, he told the lifeboat to take our stronger towline. Tom assumed charge of our vessel. He kept our stern pointing towards the yacht while the lifeboat dragged our towline to the yacht. I had put on my diving suit, ready for any emergency.

Once the towline was secured on the yacht, Tom gingerly opened the throttle. The slack was taken up and the yacht ran her engine at full power to aid us. Gently Tom increased the power. The yacht began to budge. Tom reduced power to let the weight of our vessel work for us. Slowly the yacht edged towards deeper water and soon was on an even keel, following in our wake.

We towed the yacht clear of the rocks. I radioed the skipper that we would tow him to our sheltered anchorage. There I dived down to his hull to see if there was any damage. Some anti-fouling had rubbed off and there were a few scrapemarks, but nothing more.

We learnt that the stock of the yacht's anchor had broken during the gusty dawn winds. Before they had had time to set another anchor, the vessel was aground. The family of four panicked.

'Gentlemen, what do I owe you?' the skipper, a Londoner, asked.

Tom said there was no bill. The family's eyes widened. They were expecting a hefty salvage fee.

'One day you will help another seafarer. Do for him what we did for you, without charge,' I said, remembering the words of the man in San Francisco. I had begun to repay my debt.

Tom and I were great friends, but on the third morning of December, with snow on the mountains and an unbearable cold in my bones, I told him I was heading home. I had been away for almost a year and was missing my family. The next day we said goodbye. I set off for London and caught a flight to Cape Town.

Soon after arriving, I met DeWett. His new boat was a fine 43-foot craft. We spoke of the proposed voyage to the Caribbean. I told him that I wanted to sail long distance, and in a boat of my own. I was still short of funds and needed work, getting back my old job on the *Trident Cape*.

I went offshore in early January 1988 on the first crew change of the year. Little had altered aboard the *Trident Cape*. Six divers were still there from the old team. The mood on the dive station was still up and down. We had days when tempers flared, but there were also days of practical joking. Crews went on shore leave, but I stayed. After ninety days offshore, I felt the need for a holiday, and shipped out on the next crew change.

My two weeks' shore leave was hectic. In a night club I met a woman about my age. Bernie was a school teacher. She liked sailing and joined me when I visited boatyards to look at yachts, but we found none that I could afford.

Back offshore, I pushed myself harder. I was promoted and earning more money. My tours of duty were long, and when ashore, I did not squander my savings. As a non-drinker and non-smoker, there was not much to spend my money on, other than cinema tickets with Bernie.

In mid-May the company fell into financial difficulties. Earlier in the year, another vessel had been acquired. Cutbacks had to be made until the second ship began finding diamonds and could pay its own way. Seventeen men were made redundant, and those of us who were kept on had to take on more responsibilities. I had to work on the bridge as a watch-keeper and radio operator. I liked my additional jobs and the bridge crew taught me a lot. The days were longer and harder, but I kept going.

Time passed quickly. Seventy days later, I took another shore leave. DeWett sailed for the Caribbean without me. No matter how much I would have liked to go with him, if I wanted a yacht of my own, there were sacrifices to make.

4

A DREAM REALISED

Cape St John's light flashed on my northern horizon. I was twenty days into the race, and making satisfactory progress. I beat into a fresh south south-westerly wind. In the stiff breeze I was pumping the bow compartment more frequently. Every time the *Stella-r* bounced off a wave, the water came in that bit faster through the crack in the bow left by the lump of ice.

Across the Atlantic, I did not catch a single fish. Was the Atlantic Ocean so overfished that it had nothing to offer a lone yachtsman? Terns were constantly diving into the water to feed and every day since leaving land I had seen dozens of birds. They were intrigued by my fishing lures skimming on the surface fifteen feet behind the boat and they would swoop down thinking the lures were small fish. Twice birds ended up with the hook in their beaks.

Stella-r sailed along at a rate of knots, towing the poor birds in the wake. The birds extended their wings, as if they were being towed as a glider plane. I brought them onto the deck where the exhausted creatures sat. With gloved hands, I removed the hooks. When they were freed, one or two pecked me on the hand, drawing blood, before flying off. The birds appeared fine after their ordeal, gliding astern. Soon they were back at the game of trying to catch the lure, so I pulled in the lines.

On 29 June, I clearly heard St Lawrence Radio on the VHF radio. I was sailing close to the Canadian coast to make radio contact with the St Lawrence Coast Guards. I made a ship-to-shore phone call to a friend, Mark Schrader, in Seattle. When I told him about my difficulties, he encouraged me to keep racing as best as I could manage, reminding me that I had come a long way from when he and I had first met in the autumn of 1989. That conversation restored my confidence.

***

It was eight months following Dawn Diamond's closure that I met Mark in California after sailing across the Atlantic. Without work in Cape Town, I took an unpaid job, but with all my expenses paid, aboard a 52-year-old gaff-rigged boat, the *Colin Archer*, bound for the Texas. The owner needed a delivery skipper.

My route took three crew and myself via Brazil and the Caribbean. It was an interesting voyage which came to an abrupt end in Cozumel, Mexico. The boat had been damaged in a storm. I decided to go to Cozumel to carry out repairs before crossing the Gulf of Mexico, but I had no visa for Mexico. The immigration officials would not allow me to enter their country. I was given the choice to sail on, or fly out. To sail across the Gulf of Mexico with a severely leaking boat was suicidal. I could not risk the lives of my American crew, who did not need a visa for Mexico, and was left with no option but to fly to Houston, Texas, where one of the crew lived. He gave me his front door key and told me to wait for him until he and the others brought the boat back with the owner to Galverston.

Since my savings were nearly exhausted, I needed to work immediately, and applied for work with a Houston-based diving company. I was interviewed by an operations manager, who told me there was no work. While I was in his office, a diving crew arrived after just completing a job. One of them looked familiar and he recognised me from the Diamond Coast. We had met twice in Port Nolloth.

Art Frankil was from near Cape Town, but had married a doctor from Houston. He invited me home for a drink. His wife remembered seeing me in the small town. While we were chatting, their phone rang. A jack-up oil platform had capsized off Freeport, Texas. Two bodies were missing. Art told me to return to the office with him, as Offshore Diving and Salvage had the contract to try to recover the trapped bodies.

Back at the office, he introduced me to the owner of the company, whom I asked for work. Because the situation had changed, I was temporarily hired and put on stand-by. A fellow diver going offshore with Art gave me his pager. The operations manager sent me home to pack a sea bag and be ready to go offshore at any time.

The following day I was paged. Drill mud containing oil particles had been spilt on the seabed from an oil platform. Before the coast guards spotted the source of the minor oil leak, the drilling company wanted it sucked up and disposed of properly. Since I had been involved in sub-sea mining, it was the job to send me out on, though I had no underwater duties. That job lasted a week. I dressed the diver and handled the diving-related umbilical and air supply. The work was in shallow water and required a little decompression in the water. The days were long; often we worked through the night to get the job done.

For three months after that first job, I was kept busy on oil platforms. We would be offshore for a few days, then back on land for a day or two, during which time I saw the crew of the *Colin Archer*, who had had a safe passage to America. Soon I was promoted and earning a good wage, most of which I saved.

I loved the work, but saw the damage that was being done to the environment. Supply ships were dumping their non-biodegradable waste like plastics overboard because they had no incinerators and could not store it until they went ashore. There were constant small oil spills, on which chemicals were sprayed to camouflage the oil.

The companies were interested only in profits. When a careless accident killed a partner and almost took my life too, I felt it was time to leave diving. We were working in 200 feet of water cutting pipes that pumped mud into a well. An explosion occurred when my partner cut into a pipe that contained a flammable gas. I was quite a distance away at the diving cage getting more cutting rods. Had I been cutting beside my partner, I too would have been killed instantly.

When I handed in my notice, I was given two outstanding salary cheques. Both bounced. I was not going to leave America without my money, so I visited friends in California while a lawyer tried to recover what was due to me. Eventually it appeared that I was wasting my time and would have to forget about the money I was owed.

In California, a good friend gave me a place to stay, a computer and the use of a car. I tried to raise sponsorship for a boat I had designed. Hundreds of letters were written and phone calls made seeking money and gear, all to no avail.

The Long Beach Boat Show was in October. With friends, I strolled around the show for an hour until we came to the Monitor windvane stand. I had used several windvane systems when sailing on different boats, but was impressed with the robustness of the Monitor windvane. It was my dream to have one for my transatlantic race, but it was more than I could afford.

Listening to me speaking to a friend, the Monitor salesman asked where I was from. He was Mark Schrader, the first American to solo circumnavigate the globe under sail in 1980, and a competitor in the 1986-87 BOC solo around the world race. On both voyages he spent a lot of time in Cape Town. He was the race director for the 1990-91 BOC race.

Mark was interested in knowing how I had learned about windvanes and boats, explaining that he had not met a dark-skinned South African who was keen on sailing. I explained that my ambition was to take part in the solo transatlantic race in 1992. With three years to prepare, I felt I had a chance to do it. Already I had put some money aside to begin building a boat. Mark invited me to Seattle to meet people who might help. It was the beginning of a lasting friendship. Ever since we have met once a year.

I returned to Cape Town at the end of 1989, having sailed more than 8,000 miles. I had written to the Royal Cape Yacht Club, expressing my interest in the solo transatlantic race and was invited to lunch by a committee member. Another gentleman, who was a journalist, was also invited to lunch. It was not until during lunch that I remembered that it was about ten years previously that I had met this person in a supermarket, when I started out in sailing.

Despite not being paid for the last two months' work in America, I had saved sufficient money to begin constructing a 38-foot boat. When I was diving for Dawn Diamonds, I had visited a man in Mossel Bay. Marinus Goolouze was a Dutch mathematician who had married a black woman from the area; the town disliked him for crossing the colour line.

I heard about Marinus through a magazine article. He looked at my drawings and asserted that my dream could be achieved. He modified the lines I had drawn and did a structural analysis on his computer of potential stresses and weights of the boat in fibre glass, and then in cold-moulded wood. To build in fibre glass would be expensive because a mould would have to be built first. Cold-moulded wood using epoxy was slightly cheaper and would be a stronger structure.

Marinus agreed to help me build the boat for a fee. I chose the cold-moulded method, which means bending veneers of okume, a type of wood related to the Filipino mahogany family, over a cheap wooden skeleton. The veneers are temporarily secured to the frame. Then a second layer of wood is bent over the first layer at 45 degrees and is bonded with epoxy resin, using staples to hold the shape. Once the epoxy has cured, the staples are removed and a third layer of wood is bent over the last layer at 90 degrees to the initial layer, and glued with epoxy. Three layers of wood are adhered to form the contours of the hull. Fillers are applied before the hull is sanded to the perfect shape before a layer of fibre glass is applied to give the wood a protective surface and additional strength. It was laborious work. Four people were hired to help. Once the hull was complete, the structure was turned over and the wooden skeleton taken out. Bulkheads were laminated and water ballast tanks fitted. We then began to put on the side decks and I moved into my new home aboard the boat.

One day a journalist from London arrived in Mossel Bay. He wanted to interview me. We planned to lunch at the local yacht club, where I had reciprocal membership as a member of Royal Cape Yacht Club. It was not a particularly busy afternoon in the Mossel Bay Sailing Club. The barman even had time to play a game of snooker. We took a table overlooking the harbour, and waited to have our order taken. The Afrikaans-speaking manager came over, abruptly asking if he could help us. We began to give him our lunch order when he told us in an uncivil manner that this was a private club for members only. I produced my Royal Cape Yacht Club membership card, proving that I was a member of another yacht club where anyone from their club was welcome. He pointed to the sign above the bar which stated that the rights of admission were reserved, and stood aside to see us to the door. Humiliated, we left, overhearing the barman say that it was a sad day that another club allowed 'coloured people privilege to their sport'.

Angry, I returned to Cape Town. I was saddened to see such attitudes among people of the sea who had a common interest. In Cape Town I called on equipment suppliers. A British manufacturer of electronics and autopilots offered me a forty percent discount. I went to their local distributor with a list of deck fittings and electronics to do a deal. They were willing to give me fifteen percent discount off the fittings, and what was agreed on the electronics, but I had to guarantee that I was going to make it to the start of the race. Without a sponsor, I could not give that guarantee, so they would not give me the discount.

I went to the company's competitor, explaining my predicament. The owner of Central Boating was also at the time commodore of the Royal Cape Yacht Club, a man who had encouraged my sailing. His salesman went through my lists and advised me on the options and the available make of gear. Eventually a package containing winches, deck fittings and electronics was created to suit my budget. I was assured that it would all stand up to the demands of solo racing in the North Atlantic. Without any fuss, I was give forty percent discount on Robertson Stowe electronics, a very good brand. The only guarantee asked of me was to try my best to enter the race, and keep Central Boating informed. The autopilots previously bought in London at the retail price all failed before I had reached the starting line.

I was still determined to find a sponsor. Some companies gave me a hearing; others put my proposal aside. One company chairman had the audacity to ask me what a black man would know about sailing. My blood boiled. I got up and left. Before closing the door, I turned and said, 'Obviously more than you do about people, business and the spirit of adventure, sir.'

I did send this man a letter from the finish line, reminding him of his question, and saying that since our meeting, I had sailed a further 17,000 miles solo to achieve my goal, without his help.

These rejections did not discourage me. Rather, they fuelled my resolve to find alternative ways. I turned to friends within the marine industry to sell me what I needed as cheaply as they could. Manex Marine sold me all my rigging at cost price and North Sails sold me a selection of sails at the old price.

My boat still needed a mast and a keel. I approached a mast manufacturing company, but their lowest price was outside my budget. I looked at a few damaged masts that could be shortened to fit, but they were too heavy. In the end, I met a former employee who was starting a competition business in mast manufacturing. Peter Kemp helped me find a mast section. I calculated the sail area, and we began building a mast with the agreement that he would complete it for a nominal fee.

A naval architect, who had conceived a radical sixty footer which had been entered for the previous BOC race, also designed a 35-foot version of that vessel. She had an interesting bulb keel that, if it was made deeper, would suit my boat. He gave me permission to use his design, free of charge, and I hired the mould to cast the keel.

Financially it was a struggle. My mother was good to me. I lived rent free at home. She fed me, paid the high telephone bills without complaint and lent me her car. When I got frustrated, she consoled me.

Dad was very supportive of my project, giving me pocket money to go to the movies. He too offered me encouragement, and drove me to Mossel Bay, 350km from Cape Town, to deliver gear.

I was dating several girls, but none seriously. They had to settle for walks on the beach and on Table Mountain, very simply cooked meals and the cheapest seats in the movies.

One night at a party at Bernie's home in Cape Town I met Alison, a dancer and artist eight years older than me. Bernie was happy for me when a serious romance with Alison developed. It was not an easy relationship in South Africa because Alison was from a different racial group. She was classified as 'white' by the government. We spent our weekends together, seldom going out because neither of us had money to spare and we found it difficult to deal with the stares that some people gave us.

Alison was a land lubber and did not shared my ambitions of crossing oceans. Yet she knew that sailing would separate us.

With all the purchases made, I spent most of my time in Mossel Bay. The inside of the boat was spartan; it contained a basic navigation station, a small galley where I fitted a camping gas burner, and a bench, up against one of the water ballast tanks. The bench was a workplace by day, and my bunk at night.

Once the deck had been painted, I installed the deck fittings. I designed the boat so that it could be sailed single-handed. I did the simple plumbing and wiring and, installed the two basic speed and wind electronic instruments. I worked around the clock. Every day I felt a small sense of achievement.

The keel, which I had moulded in Cape Town, was delivered to my home. I completed its modifications and made it ready to be bolted on. It was then delivered to Mossel Bay. I had planned to launch the boat there and to do sea trials before setting sail for Cape Town.

Finally in October 1990 the *Stella-r* was wheeled out of the shed on the back of a truck. It had been a job to hand-winch the boat high enough to drive the low bed truck beneath her, and lash down the hull for transportation. The keel was placed beside the hull and together it was driven the 8km to the harbour.

There had been delays along the way, but the real difficulties began when the boat was sitting at the water's edge. The protruding 10cm long keel bolts did not line up with the holes. When Peter Kemp, who also made the spacer box to deepen the draft, welded on the bolts, they became distorted. I had made a template which fitted the top of the bolts, but did not check to see that it was uniform all the way to the top of the lead. The easiest solution was to widen the holes through the hull. Eventually the keel and the boat were mated.

My boat sat in a borrowed cradle, awaiting its mast. Two weeks later the mast arrived, but all the end fittings to support the rigging had not been crinted on and it could not be rigged.

The difficulties weighed heavily on my shoulders. I was in a strange town without transport. Obtaining the right gear to complete the boat properly meant bringing everything from Cape Town. It was easier to transport the boat to Cape Town. An opportunity presented itself when a Transvaal-built yacht was launched in Mossel Bay and the transporter was travelling back to Cape Town empty. I paid them to take my boat to Cape Town.

The yacht was launched in November 1990 at the Royal Cape Yacht Club. There was no funfair. She just slipped quietly into the water. A week later the mast was erected and the rigging adjusted to keep the it in column. The base of the mast required additional support to spread the loads. The loads transferred from the keel also needed to be spread across a greater area. These were serious oversights in our design.

At this time the third BOC race had stopped in Cape Town. I had met many of the skippers the previous January when Mark invited me to attend the press launch at the Earl's Court Boat Show in London. It was at the show that I met Robin Davies, who was preparing to sail *Global Exposure* in the 1990-91 BOC race. He and I became good friends. When he sailed into Cape Town second in his class, I stopped work on my boat for a few days to help him. I was sad when the fleet sailed off without me, but I had promised myself that I would be in the next race in 1994.

Finally the day arrived when most of the jobs on my boat were complete. John Joseph, who worked in the yacht club, helped me stick the name on the hull the night before the official launch and cover it over. Numerous friends gathered for the official launching ceremony. Mark presented me with a bottle of specially labled BOC champagne and presided over the formalities. My parents were aboard the *Stella-r*, with about sixty guests on the dockside.

The cork was popped into the crowd when I opened the champagne and I gave the bottle to my mother with which to bless the boat. It was only then that I told her the name, unveiling the *Stella-r*. I named the boat after her. Without her, my dream would have been impossible. The letter *r* was the first letter of a young lady's name with whom I had been hopelessly in love ten years before. Had she felt the same way about me then, I wondered if I would have become the sailor I was. I had invited her to the launch. René came with her husband and six-year-old son. I did not publicly disclose what the last letter in my boat's name signified, but waited to tell her when we were on our own. She showed joy, shyness and embarrassment. What I felt for her all those years ago still caused uneasiness between us.

The following day three crew and I went out on our maiden voyage. A gentle breeze blew over the flat bay. Majestic Table Mountain loomed over us, reaching into the clear blue summer skies. It was an ideal day to be on the water. We put up all the sail that the *Stella-r* could carry. Our speed climbed to a steady 6 knots sailing near to the wind. I felt like a king. The Rothmans' regatta was only two weeks away, and I felt that it would be good fun to enter the *Stella-r*. A crew of seven were selected and we began training.

On the day of the first race in mid-December, we had a premature start and had to return. With sixty boats on the same starting line, we could not turn around quickly. When we did restart, we were left far behind. It was fun, although we came last.

The wind blew strongly on the second day of the series. On our way to the start, we pounded into the sea and the support beneath the mast sheared a weld. The rigging went slack as the mast base drove a longitudinal crack in the hull, letting in water. On our return to the harbour, with one of the crew monitoring the flow of water coming in through the hull, we met a gust of wind. I pulled hard on the fibre glass tiller. We heard a crack and felt the boat go out of control. The tiller had broken. With shortened sail, we managed to get the boat safely into the harbour using a piece of timber as a makeshift tiller.

I spent that Christmas with *Stella-r* out of the water. The crack had to be ground out with a sanding machine. Then the wood had to be laminated with fibre glass to get it back into its original shape. Marinus sold me some epoxy resin, which did not cure properly. It was a nightmare. Every day I went down to work onboard and had to borrow money off my mother to get it done.

While *Stella-r* was out of the water, a yachtsman from the club walked up to me. He told me that the best advice he could give a fellow sailor was to sell my heap of junk and get out with what I could. He predicted that I would never have the money to race my own vessel, but that if I were smart, I would remain crewing for wealthy yachts-men who could afford the cost of the sport.

It is easy to kick a man when he is down. I thought how sad his life must be, feeling the need to discourage a fellow sailor, when encouraging words were as easily spoken. Coming from a wealthy family, he had been given most things in life, including his boat, but he lacked the compassion to understand the power of a dream.

I was so discouraged at so many people's negative attitudes that when my vessel was launched and sea trials proved that *Stella-r* was safe enough go sailing, I left to sail around the Cape of Good Hope. Maybe in False Bay I would find goodwill. The rumours in Cape Town were that my vessel was unsound, and would not make Europe, let alone complete the transatlantic race.

In False Bay I found a different attitude. The False Bay Yacht Club gave me free mooring and the use of their club facilities. I was invited to participate in their club racing and they did what they could to help me prepare for sailing to England. My second cousin, Carl, helped crew for me. I raced the boat numerous times against larger boats, and took line honours.

Preparing to sail from Simonstown
Photographer: Roger February

A last hug from Mom.
Photographer: Roger February

On 10 February 1991 I set sail solo for Walvis Bay above the Tropic of Capricorn. Thereafter I would leave the African coast for the Azores and then sail to England to compete in the 1992 solo transatlantic race. That Sunday morning, John Joseph, who had given me tremendous support over the months, and a few close friends, joined my family and me for breakfast in the club house, while another yachtsman, John Claustra, offered to tow me out, and take my family aboard his home-built boat to see me off.

Setting off to realise my dreams.
Photographer: Roger February

The wind howled and rain squalls were coming in. At breakfast I had said to my mother that I would wait a few days for the weather to improve, but when I saw the crowd gathering, I realised that the time had come to set sail. In spite of the bad weather, numerous friends came down to bid me farewell.

At 11:00 a naval strike craft came to the pontoon and stood by. This was my surprise escort from a few yacht club members. I began making my farewells. Roger February, an old school friend, captured those moments on camera.

It was an emotional departure. When the time came for me to cast off, Alison was on the dock to help untie my mooring lines. I held her in my arms. Nearly a year had past since we had met. The previous day, I had asked her not to wait for me in the hope that I would return, because I could not guarantee that I would keep that promise. Our relationship ended four months afterwards.

It was harder to say goodbye to my parents. There was a lump in my throat. My mother was fighting back the tears. Dad was as proud as ever. Mamma, who was our neighbour who had helped raise me, was there to give me a cake she had baked; right up to the last minute she was looking after the well-being of my appetite. My sister could not make it down to see me off since it was costly to fly from Johannesburg for a weekend.

My mooring lines were slipped, as John Claustra took me under tow. The dock that I sailed from was the same dock where, eleven years before, I was a starry-eyed kid looking for my first sail. As I cleared the dock, the yacht club fired a three gun salute. I fought back the tears. I was not one of their members, but they had done so much for me.

***

Talking to Mark on the radio telephone via St Lawrence Radio awoke many joyful feelings.

The wind switched to the south-west. I beat my way down the Nova Scotia coast towards Sable Island. It was still foggy. The bird life was more abundant as we approached the Sable Banks, sailing inshore of the island that marked one area of the banks. Soon the dolphins were back playing around *Stella-r*.

Earlier in the race, my space frame, which carries the loads from the shrouds to the base of the keel, had broken. On the starboard tack, the shrouds were pulling the chainplates, which attach the rigging to the hull, out through the deck. The rigging on the port side would become very slack and come away from the spreaders. Before I could tack, I had to climb the mast to the top spreader to tie the rigging back in place. It was a nerve-racking experience to leave the deck and I dreaded hauling myself up hand over hand to the spreaders.

Whenever I was on the starboard tack with the wind coming across the starboard side of *Stella-r*, I was careful not to carry too much sail. I reefed the main sail early. My fear was that too great a load could rip out the chainplate, dismasting my vessel. When the yacht pounded hard into the sea, I held my breath. It was hard on the vessel, but even harder on my nerves.

Inshore of Sable Island, the fog finally cleared. Blue skies shone, charging my batteries via a solar panel that converted the sunrays into electric energy. I have no engine on the *Stella-r*, and rely on a solar panel. I did carry a small generator, but it was unreliable.

I sped towards the finish, still some 600 miles away. A large tail broke the surface near the boat. A mink whale dived. Several more times that day I noticed the whales playing less than a mile from *Stella-r.*

The wind freshened. The genoa had to be taken in. I secured it to the deck as *Stella-r* sailed along in a flat sea with a reef in the main, and a staysail set. Returning to the cockpit, my eye fell on the water ahead where a dark shape was looming. I was sailing towards it. It was just visible below the surface, less than ten feet deep. I froze. Seconds later, before I had time to react, *Stella-r* was over it, when I realised that it was a whale calf. Its tail was on the starboard, and its head on the port side. It was surfacing. I braced myself for the impact when the keel would strike its body, but nothing happened.

The whale must have realised that an obstruction was overhead. These animals have well-advanced instincts to detect danger. It turned and surfaced parallel to my boat, dousing me in spray from its exhaled breath. The breath had a fish-like stench.

There have been a few instances where whales have attacked vessels. Most incidents of vessels being damaged by whales happened when the mammal was asleep on the water's surface, and had been run down by a passing vessel. I do not regard whales as dangerous animals, and am more fearful of collisions with man-made objects, like ships or container crates.

5

DISASTER

On 1 July 1992 I celebrated my twenty-first day into the race. During the night, the wind increased to between 35 and 40 knots. Three reefs were in the mainsail, with the number four genoa up, instead of the smaller staysail. I was pleased with my progress towards Newport, 560 miles away, and went below deck to sleep.

A change in the boat's motion awoke me. *Stella-r* was sailing sluggishly. She should have been flying over the waves. On deck I found the number four head sail torn along its seams. I took it down, replacing it with the staysail. The boat now was moving even more slowly.

During the early hours of the morning, the wind changed direction. The sea increased as I beat into it. I tacked at daybreak towards the Nova Scotia coast, picking up garbled weather reports on the radio from Halifax. The coastal station was just out of radio range, but later in the morning I was able to put in a call to South Africa to Graham Lizamore, a journalist who had written about my sailing. I gave him my latest progress report, which he published in the weekend paper, and contacted my family to tell them I was well.

Towards afternoon, the wind eased off and came back onto my beam. I dearly missed the number four sail. There was insufficient wind to carry the staysail, but too much for the number three sail. Still, I slogged along. After sunset the wind increased. I kept sailing towards the Canadian coast, spotting Beaver Island lighthouse, followed by Liscomb lighthouse, during the night. The loom of reflective orange light on the clouds of an unknown city was evident on my western horizon. I was now very close to the coast. My nerves became frayed, worrying that

I would fall asleep and run aground. I was badly in need of rest, not having had a good sleep for more than two days.

An hour later, I felt that I was pushing my luck too far, tacking off the coast. It was a wise decision. Soon the wind freshened, creating a lumpy sea. A weather depression engulfed the area, causing strong westerly winds followed by thunder and lightning. It got too rough to carry the mainsail, so I took it down in the pouring rain, the seas breaking over the boat. I was very cold.

***

Eighteen months earlier, I had experienced similar weather. I had sailed from Simonstown, just outside Cape Town, leaving behind friends and family, bound for Port Nolloth, my first stop. En route I encountered a severe gale, running ahead of it with only a staysail. For two days it was too rough to cook a meal or to rest. I was close to the coast, but could not see it for the fog. When the gale past, the fog intensified and I was left becalmed for a day until the weather changed.

I sailed into the diamond capital of the west coast during the late afternoon. Little had changed in Port Nolloth. The same racists still lived there, denying me access to their only restaurant, even though the South African government had claimed that the country's political situation was improving.

I invited a few friends from the town to dine on my humble home. Present was a diver who had worked with me on the *Trident Cape*, a lead diver for the first company who had hired me, but now had his own diamond mining boat and was employing other divers to work for him, and three deckhands who tried to teach me Afrikaans five years before. It was a delightful evening entertaining my former colleagues aboard *Stella-r*.

A week later I sailed 150 miles north to Luderitz, in Namibia. I stayed there for three months, enjoying the intense desert heat and working on my boat. Ian Wingate from the *Trident Cape* became the harbourmaster after Dawn Diamonds shut its doors. He welcomed me to the architectural Gothic town, caught between the desert and the deep blue sea, situated on the shores of five lagoons. Namibia was once a German colony, and Luderitz had been influenced by German architecture.

Three Spanish trawlers, caught for illegal fishing, were in one of the lagoons. Eight trawlers were to take up residence in the lagoon while I was there; their captains were imprisoned and the vessels were confiscated. Their arrival caused quite a stir in the quiet town which rarely saw that number of ships in the lagoon simultaneously. The vessels generated some maintenance and security work for the local population who were dependent upon the dying diamond and crayfish industries.

I sailed to the surrounding bays. In Hottentot Bay, thirty miles north, I watched a rhebok, a South African antelope, walk into the sea and stand with only its head and antlers above the water.

On another trip to that bay, I rowed ashore and spent hours walking among the dunes, finding different animal tracks. I followed one set of spoor, and soon came across wild desert horses, roaming free. There must have been hundreds of horses together, living off the dew formed on the few blades of very tough grass that managed to survive there. I later learnt from some naturalists whom I met in the town, that hyenas lived in the region, feeding on gull eggs.

I left *Stella-r* in Luderitz harbour for a few weeks and hitched a lift home to see my family and Alison. The bonds between Alison and me had not diminished during my absence. My mother and Ralf Freeze, a friend and former student of my mother's, returned with me to Luderitz. Ralf drove us and decided to sail with us to Walvis Bay, a South African enclave in Namibia and part of the Cape Province. He and I had done a lot of work aboard *Stella-r* in Luderitz to prepare for the ocean crossing from Walvis Bay. We left in early May and had a slow windless sail. We drifted north on the cold northerly-flowing Benguela current that sweeps up the south-western coast of Africa from the Antarctic Ocean, enriching the coast with plankton.

On 1 June 1991, after Ralf had left, my sister Jan, whom I had not seen for a year, flew into Walvis Bay for two days. I was leaving the African coast for the Azores. Jan said that the cost of seeing me outweighed the expense of the short trip. The following morning Mom, Jan and I rose early. The day for my departure had arrived. I felt apprehensive about the voyage. It was such a huge undertaking.

After breakfast, we went to the morning service at the Seamen Mission. It was the first time in ten years that we had gone to church as a family — we are not a religious family. After church, I rang my father to say goodbye; then Alison. Down on the dock, I shook hands with a few people I had met in Walvis Bay. It was hard saying goodbye to my mother and sister. I felt the tears welling up, and could see the shine of tears in Jan's eyes, but we would not let them flow. I reserved mine for the privacy of the bay, where I wept for some time.

Once alone, I tethered my self to the boat with a safety harness, so that should I fall over board, I would be able to pull myself back onboard. The next day, 3 June, I celebrated my twenty-fourth birthday alone at sea. It was lonely, but I had to adjust to being on my own. I missed my family, friends and Alison, but the duties on board kept me busy. Every day I had routine jobs to do. I breakfasted on cereal, walked around the deck looking at the sails and rigging, did the last of the coastal navigation as I was losing sight of land, read a few pages of *David Copperfield* and cooked a main meal. During the voyage I also read short stories by Joseph Conrad and James Missioner's *Alaska* and *The Covenant*.

I took out my books on celestial navigation, and began to study the things that Ian Windgate had taught me on the *Trident Cape*. I took my first sighting of the sun through a sextant on the second morning, soon after the land had disappeared over the horizon. A sextant is an optical instrument that measures the angle of a heavenly body in relation to the horizon. Applying the exact time the sight is taken, in a trigonometry formula, the sailor's latitude and longitude can be calculated. The sun and other selected stars, the planets and the moon all can be used, but I chose the sun, the easiest one to find.

When I had taken my first sighting, and made the calculation, the result put me in another ocean! I checked and rechecked the calculation, referring to the textbook, but still got the same result. I began to worry; this was my only means of navigation! My budget did not allow me the luxury of a satellite or other electronic navigation system. I persisted taking sightings until I found the error in my method. I had taught myself the art of celestial navigation, using the sun as my heavenly body.

My schooldays seemed so far away, but I could apply the knowledge I had gained over those twelve years to make my voyage possible. Without arithmetic, I would not have been able to calculate how much stores and water I would need for a given journey, knowing the expected length of the passage and my approximate consumption of the item of food and liquid. Geography had taught me about the climates of the countries I would visit, which oceans swept past their shores, the currents, tides and winds I would encounter. If, as a student, I had been made to understand where each educational component fitted in the global sphere of learning, school would have been exciting.

I found the south-east trade winds and made good progress. On the sixth day out, my generator would not start. I had no other means of charging my batteries to run the electronic autopilot. The trade winds freshened as *Stella-r* raced towards the Azores. I helmed some of the time, but when I needed rest, the autopilot took over. I was debating whether to call at the island of St Helena, six hundred miles north and off my route, but considering the exorbitant landing costs I was told about by other sailors, thought I would first try to repair the generator.

The days became weeks. I settled down to a set daily routine. There were no ships to be seen. Ahead lay an entirely new world. I was nine hundred miles from Walvis Bay. Little was I to know how it would turn into a different way of life.

Two days later a decision was made for me when the autopilot's electronics began giving trouble. It made a strange noise and stopped working. I altered course for St Helena. Desperate to have some form of self-steering, I opened the autopilot, but could not find anything wrong. When it was assembled, it worked. I continued, deciding to helm some of the time and to use the autopilot only when I wanted to sleep or prepare a meal.

I found it hard going and was constantly tired. Lonely and homesick, I desperately wanted to talk to my mother. Something was bothering me, but I did not know what it was, except that talking to Mom, I knew, would ease my mind. I considered sailing within range of St Helena radio, but due to a wind shift, I overshot the island.

When I had been at sea for nearly three weeks with no one to talk to, one night I sighted a light on the horizon. I tried to call up the vessel on the radio, but with no success. Then it disappeared. During the day I sighted a large factory ship, which I presumed to be the light I had seen. Again I tried to call it on the radio, but without luck. I altered my course to pass very close to the ship, hoping that someone on board would see me.

The ship sailed past and disappeared over the horizon. I was angry. I needed to speak to another human being who, I hoped, would give me encouragement.

On 22 June, a day after sighting the ship, I crossed the Equator and sailed into the Northern Hemisphere. It had taken me twenty days to reach latitude zero. Still benefiting from the south-east trade winds, I altered course sixty degrees towards the north-east, a course which should have taken me about 100 miles west of the Cape Verde Islands.

Accompanying me across the equator were eight bonito, a fish similar to tuna. Each was of a size that would make a delicious meal. The fish avoided my two fishing lines that trailed from the stern. Instead, I ate the last of the bananas and a can of vegetable curry. My meals at sea varied from flying fish, a delicacy that occasionally landed on the deck, to chocolate. The flying fish would leap out of the waves, spread their lateral fins like wings and propel themselves out of the water to glide into the breeze. At night I hung a lantern in the cockpit so that my boat was visible to any shipping. The light attracted the flying fish, which landed on the deck. In the mornings I gathered more than half-a-dozen fish, cleaned and beheaded them, and cooked them in a pan. They made a lovely, simple breakfast.

The lines were not left out all the time; only when I wanted fish. I also caught tuna fish. If it was too large, or too small, it was returned to the ocean. Baked in the oven, tuna made a filling meal. When dorado, also known by the Spaniards as Dolphin fish, was caught, it was promptly returned to the ocean. Dorado mated for life. Kill one, and in time its partner will die too. I adopted the philosophy that if you looked after the sea, the sea would take care of you.

My meals were dependent upon the state of the sea. When the weather was calm, they were elaborate. I would cook pasta, with onions, garlic and canned tomatoes fried in fruit chutney. When moderate weather came, it would be boiled potatoes with melted cheese. In rough weather, I did not cook; the risks of spilling something hot onto me was too great. Instead, I ate lots of nuts, raisins and chocolate. I did crave to have steak, but, most of all, ice cream.

In the warmth of the tropical sun, ninety miles north of the Equator, I sweltered on deck dreaming of cold ice cream. There was not a breath of wind and the sails were hanging limply. It was very hot on deck and even hotter below. Buckets of warm seawater brought temporary relief from the unforgiving sun. I scanned the horizon looking for wind, shipping and a rain squall, but the ocean was empty. Several times I considered taking a swim, but was afraid of what might be lurking in the water.

Music blared loudly from inside the cabin. I listened to the songs of the Beatles, The Police, Neil Diamond, Michael Jackson and the Beach Boys. On deck I peeled one of my rapidly diminishing supply of oranges. The biodegradable skin was tossed overboard.

I stood up, naked except for my harness which tethered me to the boat, to look again at the horizon. There appeared to be some cloud formation to the south-west. Then I saw the boom speeding towards me. I tried to duck but was not quick enough and it hit my head. I was swept across the deck, but my harness stopped me from falling overboard. I landed on the opposite side of the cockpit, ten feet away. Dazed, I rose onto wobbly legs to see a blurred world spinning about me.

There was blood on the deck. It was spurting from my left eyebrow. The sight of blood made me giddy and nauseous, and I had to sit down. I sat bleeding for probably twenty minutes, before finding the strength to go below deck for the medical kit. By applying pressure to the wound, I reduced the bleeding. Using salt water, I cleaned the wound. My eyebrow had swollen and the eye was closed.

With my good eye, I squinted into a mirror. I nearly passed out! The bone along the inch slit in my skin was visible. Again a dizzy spell gripped me. I was afraid now. The wound needed to be stitched, but the nearest doctor was in the Cape Verde Islands, 1,700 miles distant. I was alone on a small yacht in a huge ocean, with no wind and no long range radio to summon help.

Tears came to my good eye. Was I going to die from the loss of blood, or lose my eye because there was no medical help? I knew it was up to me. The wound had to be closed and I could do it. Stitching it in a mirror with shaky hands and on a rolling yacht was out of the question.

I decided to use a clothes peg. I cleaned the wound as best as I could, before pinching the gapping lumps of eyebrow flesh together, and then holding them together with the clothes peg. It was not comfortable at first, but when the bleeding ceased, I was unaware of the pressure the peg put on the skin. Sleeping was awkward, because I had to lie on my back.

The swelling went down gradually, but any facial expressions could dislodge the cloths peg. I frequently removed the peg to clean around the wound. At first it would start bleeding again, but as the wound healed, it ceased. By the third day, I no longer needed the peg. The brow had knitted on its own. I still had headaches, but a week later I had forgotten about the accident.

I was fully recovered by the time, two weeks later, I went ashore on the Cape Verde Islands. Three days afterwards, *Stella-r* was back at sea, bound for Horta, in the Azores where I arrived during the first week of August. The only place to tie up was alongside a 50-foot American yacht, called *Dream Chaser*. Ron and Caroline, two doctors who went to sea to pursue their dreams, were on deck to take my lines. Once *Stella-r* was secure, I was invited aboard this luxury yacht for a drink, and offered the use of their bath, while Caroline cooked me lunch. This successful and wealthy couple had all the fancy gear aboard their floating home, shared with their three young children and a tutor.

My arrival was in time for the Festival of the Sea. The town of Horta was out celebrating. There were marquees with music, parades and dancing in the main street until the early hours. I spent two delightful weeks in the marina, tied up alongside *Dream Chaser*.

All too soon, it was time to set sail again. Early on the morning of 14 August I departed on the last leg of my voyage to Plymouth, some 1,400 miles, which I estimated would take up to twelve days. My water supplies and provisions were meant to last me two weeks, with another three days extra for safety.

The last leg began slowly in the company of a blue whale, seen sounding a mile away. The North Atlantic high pressure weather system had engulfed the islands, leaving precious little wind. My selected course was north to find the westerly winds, which would bring me towards the English Channel. Unfortunately, the wind was from the north north-east, and the best I could do was sail north-west. Progress was reasonable, and I was covering about a hundred miles a day.

On the morning of 19 August, the winds died. I bobbed about on the swell when I spotted a Russian factory ship on the horizon sailing in my direction. I raised her on the radio, but her reply was in very broken English. I was told to stand by. A few minutes later, I was called on the radio by someone who spoke good English. He explained that he was a galley hand whom the captain had sent for to translate our communication.

I requested weather information for the area, and learnt that a cold front was imminent. Before radio communications ceased, the vessel altered her course to sail close to me so that the crew could have a look at my vessel. The captain offered me fuel, but my outboard engine ran on petrol, not diesel. They stopped 10 metres away and tossed a line over to *Stella-r*. When I pulled the line aboard, I found a basket containing a half bottle of vodka, a pornographic magazine and two litres of ice cream!

Soon after the Russian ship had disappeared over the western horizon bound for its fishing grounds off the South American coast, a gentle westerly breeze blew up.

Throughout the day it freshened. I put the large head sail up, using the spinnaker pole to hold it outboard to one side, and with the mainsail on the other side, progressed towards land. By sunset, the wind had veered to the north-west and a reef was taken into the mainsail, causing only a marginal drop in speed.

The seas grew all afternoon. My auto pilot was not coping as *Stella-r* ran before the stiff breeze. Towards evening the wind rose. The barometer fell quickly, indicating an approaching gale. White horses capped the swell. *Stella-r* was screaming down the faces of the waves. She began surfing nine, ten, eleven, and then twelve knots; white water rushed down the sides of the hull as the bow parted the seas. Then the wave was past. The speed fell away, back to eight knots, nearly double what I had been sailing at since leaving the Azores.

Darkness had come. Above the mast, pinheads of light formed the constellations. No moonlight diminished the magnificence of the radiating stars. A shooting star streaked across the heavens. Here and there were a few clouds.

In the cockpit, the instrument lights were glowing. The wind was twenty-eight knots, with strong gusts. My hand tightened on the tiller and I focused on the instruments. The speed climbed — twelve, thirteen, fourteen knots. I concentrated on keeping the stern angled away from the wave. I surfed down the front of the waves... fifteen, fifteen point one, point two, point three... rapidly reeling in the miles towards Plymouth.

The spray was flying past, stinging my face. It was warm. I could feel the wind on my cheek. My heart pumped adrenalin faster. No drug could create such a tremendous feeling of sheer exhilaration and freedom. The instruments registered fifteen point four, point five, point six knots, when suddenly I became aware of an unnatural noise and a different motion.

My speed fell to below one knot. The surf-covered waves passed us by, willing us to join them, but the *Stella-r* was unresponsive. I was flung across the cockpit by a jolt from the tiller. Over the roar of the sea, I could hear the sails flogging. The boat had stopped slicing through the seas. We were out of control.

'All hands on deck,' I shouted to myself, the young solo sailor, driven by my dream.

I looked below deck to see water rising slowly! There were two holes in the deck where the mainsail sheet had ripped out the fittings. Gear was strewn across the cabin floor and water was sloshing into the bunks.

The genoa became shredded before I had a chance to get it down. The wind began to freshen to over thirty knots, with numerous black clouds veiling the night skies. No longer was my craft a seaworthy vessel.

A semi-submerged container crate which had come off a container ship had collided with *Stella-r*. This I was not to discover until the boat was lifted out of the water and deep gouge marks were noticed in the lead keel. Container crates regularly fall off ships. Mostly they remained afloat for several hours before sinking, but if they are filled with electronics that are bubble-wrapped in plastic, the crate could remain buoyant for a long time. It would float on the surface with only a few centimetres showing. In rough weather, it cannot be seen.

The damage was severe. The rudder stock had been snapped, tearing out the bearing. Water was coming in the hull from the holes on the deck and from where the keel joined the hull. I was not aware until *Stella-r* was lifted out, that a keel bolt had snapped and the hull was cracked, allowing in water. I panicked. Was she sinking? Would courage and determination be sufficient to survive?

I bailed the water out into the cockpit with a bucket. Once all the water was removed, I was able to monitor the rate at which it was coming in. Thankfully, it was not too severe. For the remainder of the voyage I bailed out water for twenty to thirty minutes every three hours, depending on the state of the sea.

On deck I lowered what remained of the genoa. The mainsail was still flogging, helplessly. There was no point trying to make a steering system until the weather improved. What I needed most was a good night's rest. I slept fitfully for six hours.

6

SOLITUDE AND
FRUSTRATION

On 3 July 1992, I had 146 miles to go to Nantucket Island, with another 120 miles beyond that to the finish line. A stiff breeze whisked me along at seven knots according to my Garmin GPS, an electronic instrument that uses the signals of several satellites orbiting the earth to calculate the position of the receiver on board the vessel. This information is updated every three seconds. From it I was able to deduce my speed. I continued to sail a very tactical race, relying on the weather information that the coastal authorities were transmitting on the VHF radio. They forecast south-east winds that afternoon. I had a stiff northerly breeze, running before it to the south. I kept going south, even though the most direct route to my destination was west-south-west. I was hoping to get north-east of Nantucket Island before the wind changed.

Instead of doing what had been forecast, the wind died and a mist came in to reduce visibility. I detected from my navigation that where I was sailing, there was a strong tide. For several hours, I struggled to make progress. Several whales passed by the boat, swimming a lot faster than I was drifting.

Near George's Bank, a slight whisper of wind helped improve visibility tremendously. Night had come. On the horizon were the deck lights of numerous vessels, which turned out to be a fishing fleet. All night I remained on deck as I sailed towards the fleet. It appeared to be travelling in the same direction as me, only more slowly. A few hours before dawn, I began overhauling the fleet, and could hear their chatter on the VHF radio, but no one seemed to hear me call. The boats altered course to come and look at *Stella-r*.

At first light I counted 28 boats around me. Looking through binoculars, I identified a name on a bow and called the vessel. She responded, but was unable to answer my questions about the tides and weather frequencies. Minutes later a different vessel called me up. *Lady of Grace* from New Bedford Harbour gave me the information I was seeking. In conversation, he also identified the whale species as Minkey and told me that the whale numbers were increasing.

I learnt that the *Lady of Grace* was fishing for hake and that they were at sea for a week at a time, before returning to the whaling port of New Bedford, Massachusetts. The skipper was concerned about the overfishing on George's Bank. Something had to be done, but he was not sure what the best solution was, short of stop fishing, which would force the fishermen into other jobs.

The *Lady of Grace* came over to have a close look at me. During the night, the skipper had spoken to another competitor, Francis Bourgeois, sailing *DDGF*, who was less than twelve hours ahead and racing in my class. The fishing boat offered me a fish for lunch, but accepting it could have disqualified me, since it would have been 'receiving outside assistance while racing'.

***

The collision with the solid object depressed me. The way to revive my spirits was to sleep. When I awoke at daybreak, I felt better, but the boat was still heaving and pitching in the rough seas and the wind was screeching through the rigging. Outside was a grey damp Atlantic sky, threatening more gales. The barometer was still low, and had fallen ten millibars overnight.

My situation was desperate. Water was sloshing in the bilge and over the floorboards as *Stella-r* continued to roll.

The transverse stringers, wooden frames laminated to the hull, which run from port to starboard to distribute the load of the keel and support the floor, were broken in the front area around the keel. The hull was structurally weaker and I risked losing the keel.

I had to get the *Stella-r* to a safe port where a rudder could be fitted. Using a bunk-board lashed to the spinnaker pole was not a bad idea, but required a lot of work. The board had to be drilled with holes so that it could be securely lashed to the pole. That task took me hours in the rolling seas. On deck it was too rough and wet to work.

I stood in the companionway hatch looking at the transom where the thirty horsepower engine was mounted on its bracket. It had to be shifted. As I was about to go below to my bunk, I sighted a ship. On the second call on the VHF radio, I raised her and was able to inform the watch officer of my situation and request a position. A few minutes later a different voice came on the air, identifying himself as the captain. He asked me for details of the leak and how I planned to steer the boat, how many crew were aboard and how many supplies I had left. Thereafter he offered to bring his ship alongside if I wanted to scuttle the *Stella-r*.

There was no need to ponder. The offer was kindly declined and the ship sailed on towards the Caribbean.

I slept in three to four hour sessions, awakening to bucket out water from the bilges. Then I wrote in my log about my difficulties and my loneliness. From the position the ship had given me, I plotted all my options on the chart. The Azores was 600 miles to the south, and astern. Brest in France was 800 miles east and the entrance to the English Channel about 950 miles away.

My diary of 22 August 1991 read:

I am on my own. I got myself into this and I am going to get out of it okay. I could turn back to Horta, but I am too proud. Good sailors do not go backwards. No, it's not pride, it's being practical. To return is the easiest option, but I know that if I go back, finding material to build the new rudder will not to be easy, or cheap. I will also risk having to stay the winter as weather in the Atlantic is becoming rough with the approach of winter. The possibility to miss the transatlantic race is too big. I have to find a port closer to the starting line. Better still, I have to make Plymouth.

My survival would depend on my mental state, and physical condition. I unpacked my food lockers to take stock of what was left. Since I had expected to be in Plymouth before the end of August, I had not brought many provisions onboard. There were seven slabs of 100g chocolate, 4kg mixed nuts and raisins, 3kg rice, 1.5kg pasta, nine cans of peach slices in syrup, one bottle of champagne, two cans of vegetarian curry, eight cans of peas, 3kg of corn flakes and two litres of long-life milk.

My drinking water supply was very different. The leg had been started with 24-litres of fresh water in five drums, but I had consumed one drum. During the gale, two drums had broken their lashings and had leaked their contents into the bilge. The third container I had nearly exhausted and, for some unknown reason, my fourth receptacle was only half full. My total water capacity was about eleven litres. My normal daily water consumption was a litre per day, but I drank more in hot weather. I would have to cut my water intake to a half litre per day, transferring the water between two drums. My cooking habits changed, because pasta and rice required plenty of fresh water.

On 23 August I spotted another ship coming from Gibraltar. It gave me a position but was unable to give me water since the seas were still very rough. The gale had pushed me seventy miles south-west in three days. The ship informed me of a high pressure system to the west, slowly drifting north-east. An hour later, the barometer rose and the weather began moderating. Blue skies were visible among the fluffy white clouds.

In the afternoon the seas had calmed to a gentle rolling Atlantic swell. Work on deck commenced with the retrieval of the heavy outboard engine from the transom. The spinnaker pole and bunk-board were bolted together and lashed as tightly as I could to the transom. It was difficult holding the awkward contraption with one hand so as not to drop it over the side, and trying to tie it together with the other hand. It took me hours. I felt I had earned a reward of a full glass of water and half a bar of chocolate.

Then I took fifteen buckets of water out of the bilge before I returned to the deck to begin sailing. First the main sail with two reefs in was hoisted, followed by the staysail. The spinnaker pole was lifted as a tiller, depressing the floating wooden board into the water. I pulled on it to fill the flogging sails. The boat bore away and gathered speed. The loads on the pole increased drastically as the boat began to accelerate. I strained my muscles to keep control. I was moving, and in the right direction, but steering was immensely difficult. It was also tiring and meant that I would have to be on the tiller helming all the time. It did give me something to do and occupied my mind, but was physically demanding. Exposed to the elements, I would need more liquid intake and better meals, of which I had insufficient stores.

An hour later, the bunk-board lashings worked their way loose and the steering system was nearly lost. My morale fell. Hours of hard work had been undone. Evening was approaching. Nothing could be done until daybreak, so I took down the sails and went to bed.

I had a nightmare. People were chasing me to chop off my toes. I was running, but could not move, looking over my shoulders to see the gap closing. I awoke in a cold sweat. Every time I closed my eyes to sleep, the nightmare came back. When my eyes were open and I lay awake, other nightmares filled my head to do with my dangerous situation. How was I going to steer my disabled craft to safety and find the money to repair it and prepare for the race? Was it worth going on?

To make matters worse, at sunrise the wind died. The barometer continued to rise as the sky turned a bright cloudless blue. The weather was really against me. If the gales did not drive me off course, the calms were going to make me insane.

The following day there was still wind. I did not bother to hoist sail. My sun sight put me more or less in the same location. My diary for 25 August 1991 reads:

I wish I could walk across the road to the café to have a doughnut and a cup of coffee. To indulge, I would love an ice cream. I miss Ron and Caroline, and the other sailors I met in Horta. They were like family.

Under normal circumstances at sea, I have always been able to cope with the isolation. I do not yearn for company, but here in the calms, hundreds of miles from anywhere, I feared that I might not see my family again.

Drifting on an empty ocean made me realise that, as John Donne said, no man is an island. Within us all are the basic instincts to survive. I wanted to survive.

The sun beat down on the boat, making it hot and clammy below deck. I did not feel like hanging out my damp sleeping bags, cooking a meal or bailing out water. For days I had not brushed my teeth, something I usually did religiously.

I sat on deck gulping a glass of water. Conserving supplies no longer mattered; I felt there would be no tomorrow. I had a second glass, and a third! When I tried to pump a fourth glass, I found that there was no more water in the barrel! I had only five litres left! In three days I had consumed half my remaining water rations, even though I had tried to get by on half a glass of water a day.

I remained on deck fighting off my drowsiness because I was afraid of the nightmares. The colours of the sky reminded me of an evening I spent with a schoolfriend, with whom ten months before I had sat on a blanket overlooking Hout Bay, in Cape Town, sipping champagne and eating cheese. At high school, when I spoke of my dream of a life at sea, she and her friends thought me crazy. Now I concluded that she had been right.

As if Nature knew that I was depressed, it sent hundreds of dolphins leaping over the western horizon, to surround the boat. Some leapt and waved their tails; others did flips. I got out the binoculars and watched the distant dolphins in groups of about ten break the surface in unison.

I suddenly forgot about my troubles. It was good to be alive. The sunset — a majestical ball of red fire sinking into an orange-coloured sea — gave me another reason to stay alive.

There had to be a way of steering a vessel without a rudder. Dinghies are often steered on sails alone, using the crew weight forward of aft on the boat to gain a direction. I could use my sails to steer!

I hoisted the mainsail and staysail. A five to seven knots breeze filled the sails and moved the boat forward until it tacked. I sheeted the staysail to lee, watching the boat creep forward and tack moments later again. Once again I sheeted the staysail on the opposite side, this time letting out the mainsail until it flogged. The boat kept moving forward without tacking, but in the wrong direction. I wanted to go east, not south-west.

What little breeze there was, came out of the west. I sheeted in the mainsail, bringing the boat onto a reach towards the north-west before the elements overpowered my vessel and the boat tacked again. Thinking about the balance of the boat, I concluded that the mainsail was driving the stern around, forcing the tack.

Before it got completely dark, and I became too engrossed in the technical side of steering, I went below to bucket out the water which had risen above the floorboards and was sloshing into my bunk. If it was not for the high-pitched squeals of the dolphins, I would not have cared about the damp bunks and the discomfort. Earlier in the day I was beyond caring, and would have slept in it, even with the water splashing in.

But the dolphins were urging me to fight and chase my dream. Slowly I began filling the bucket one scoop at a time and emptying it over the side. Twenty-one buckets were emptied. When the bilges were dry, I left the bucket in the cockpit and had a look at the sails. It was the first time that I had removed all the water from the bilges. Then an idea came to me.

I hurried below to get rope, then went onto the foredeck to fetch the spinnaker pole. On the stern, I secured the spinnaker pole perpendicular to the boat's centre line. Then I ran two ropes from each winch through ends of the spinnaker pole to the bucket.

Once this contraption had been set up, I tossed the bucket over the stern into the water. It filled and sank. Then the staysail was freed and sheeted to lee. The boat began to gather speed. I eased out rope from both winches so that the bucket dragged astern about five meters off the transom. The mainsail was eased out. As the boat gathered speed, the bucket was dragged to just below the surface, creating a disturbance in the water. The boat began moving north-west at two knots.

I fiddled with the sails until I found the best combination of how far astern and on which side of the boat to drag the bucket in relation to the trim of the sails. My course altered between northerly to north-easterly.

At last I was moving again. The dolphins stayed with me, playing near the stern by the turbulence caused by the bucket. I could hear them leaping and splashing beside the boat in the dark. It was time to get some rest. My steering system had its own self-steering gear as I maintained a northerly to north-north-easterly course to seek stronger winds.

On the first day, I covered thirty miles. My noon and afternoon sun sights were very close to each other. The monotony was broken on day 15 when a swallow landed on board. It did not appear tired and was very curious, hopping around the deck, including a brief flying visit below deck. I offered it some of my precious water, which it readily accepted. When I held out a finger, it perched itself on it for a period, then hopped back to the deck to explore the ropes. After a while it came to the conclusion that I was not going anywhere in a hurry, so it flew west. I had no clue where it had come from, but was grateful for its brief company.

On day 16 I was sitting in the cockpit reading Conrad's *Lord Jim*. It was sunny and calm. Progress had been very slow, but gradually I was approaching the Bay of Biscay. I ate the last of the nuts and raisins. There was still one chocolate slab left. Suddenly there was a snort right behind me. I jumped. A huge whale sounded less than three meters

Inside my humble home.
Photographer: R.M Goodbody

away, followed by another. Both mammals were larger than my boat. They circled me, sounding and reappearing close by. I was terrified that they would surface beneath the boat. When they were to windward of me, I could smell their fishy breath. They remained around the *Stella-r* for several hours. The boat gybed for no apparent reason. I decided to sail south-east for a day. The whales followed; neither was far from the other. They frolicked around, tail-waving and spouting, as they too enjoyed the sun.

That evening the barometer began falling steadily. At sunset the wind died, leaving my bucket to hang vertically in the water off the spinnaker pole. The whales did not hang around, but executed a tail-wave before leaving.

All night I waited for the wind and watched the barometer falling. At dawn a gentle breeze picked up from the north-east. I trimmed the boat onto an easterly heading and sailed towards the English Channel. In the late morning I put in the first reef. In the afternoon I put in the second reef. I was going well. The boat was sailing east at five knots with the bucket creating a small rooster tail astern.

During the night I had to reef again, before the weather forced me to take down the mainsail. The barometer continued to fall. At sunrise dark clouds rolled in. Three hours later the staysail was taken down. I drifted with no sails up before a forty knot wind.

The wind continued to blow strong and I grew more frustrated. Under normal circumstance with an operational rudder, I would have been making good progress towards Plymouth.

It had been several days since I had spoken to my last ship. The sky remained cloud-covered, but I was able to get a noon sight of the sun which gave me my latitude. I estimated my longitude from the time the sight was taken. I was north of the shipping lanes, but soon hoped to intersect with a ship which could give me a weather forecast.

I drifted south for two days. My exasperation increased. The periods between bucketing out the bilge water grew longer. I had not made myself a hot meal once during the gale. There was not much point going on deck. If a ship was on a collision course with me, there was nothing I could do to get out of its way, other than use the radio in the hope that its watch-keeper would respond to the call in time. Sleep was what the mind wanted; I yearned to be numbed so that I could not feel the pain of my isolation.

The following day I did look beyond the cabin from the confines of the companionway hatch. Watching the dark clouds speedily drifting across the heavens, I saw a contrail. I followed its path to find the aircraft bound towards Europe. That made me feel more depressed.Thirty thousand feet above the ocean, passengers sat in cosy seats, ate decent aircraft food and had lots to drink. They would be landing at their destination within hours. All I wanted was plenty of water to drink and to know that soon I would be safely arriving ashore.

The last leg from the Azores was supposed to be easy and fast. On day 20 out from Horta, the wind eased and the barometer began climbing rapidly. Before noon I had the sail up and was going east again. I ate my last slab of chocolate and discovered that I had only one litre of drinking water left. I suddenly felt gripped by panic. I had to further ration my water until it rained, but there was no sign of rain. A huge high pressure system was developing over the Atlantic.

The seas were still big and the wind fresh, but with three reefs in the mainsail and a staysail, I was making slow progress. It occurred to me to use the storm jib on the forestay to increase my sail area. That evening the wind freshened and the boat kept tacking itself onto a northerly heading, and I no longer cared.

To conserve batteries, I used a pump up kerosene lamp, carrying a ten litre drum of kerosene. Over the months at sea, the tin drum had corroded through. To make life more unpleasant, the kerosene had found its way into the bilge, turning the water an oily and smelly milk colour. The floorboards were slippery and dangerous. I could not be bothered to pump out the contaminated water from the bilge till the next day. It found its way into nearly everything. Weeks later, after washing out the bilge with soapy water, the smell was still there.

Slowly I closed the distance with the coast. There was still little signs of shipping other than the litter that various sailors had cast overboard. Daily I saw plastic bags, salt-shakers and other plastic containers drifting by. It felt as if I was sailing in a rubbish dump. I was disgusted. Animals ate this refuse and perished from it. Were the dolphins I had seen three days before going to become an endangered species because of mankind's selfishness?

My water was running critically low as the high pressure persisted. I was down to drinking one glass of water per day, supplementing my liquid intake with juices from the canned fruit and peas. The latter was revolting and I came to detest peas.

On the twenty-fourth night at sea, I witnessed a spectacular lightning storm. The bolts hit the water around the boat. The noise was horrendous and I was scared that a lightning bolt would strike my mast. When the storm had past, I shook out the reefs and continued on a north-easterly course. I had eaten my favourite foods and the miserly water rations left me dehydrated with a thick tongue. I felt weighed down by the weather, and by not being able to eat well.

The following dawn I awoke to find myself in fog. Everything was damp. If it rained, water could be collected, but the misty air would not yield any water. In the late afternoon I tried the radio on low power and much to my surprise, raised a ship. The watch officer had looked at the radar and had seen two objects on it. One had to be the *Stella-r*, but he was not sure which. I asked him for his position which could not have been more than 10 miles from me, and a weather forecast, which would not change for several days. An anti-cyclone had developed because of intensifying high pressure.

When I explained my predicament, the captain said that he would alter course and see if they could do anything to help. Half an hour later I heard her engines before she loomed out of the fog. She came fairly close, giving me a precise position which put me 180 miles south-west of the Fastnet Rock in County Cork. The Filipino captain offered me drinking water, but as his vessel came close to me, we realised that the swell was still too large. My mast was scribing circles in the sky and risked hitting the vessel's superstructure. Reluctantly, they wished me well and steamed off.

I wrote my encounters with the ship in my log, feeling happier for the contact. On 6 September 1991, day 25, my diary read:

Fog cleared this morning. Sunshine but cold. Trying to make Celtic Sea to get to Cork on the Irish south coast. Wind gone east, forcing me north-east. Very unusual wind. Sighted a low flying aircraft. Came low over the horizon directly towards me. I wondered if it would clear my mast. At last minute it banked to port and flew astern of me. So low that I could recognise the pilots. It flew in the direction of Ireland.

As I progressed towards the Irish coast, I saw whales in the distance. Dolphins came to play and gannets dived from incredible heights into the water after fish.

Then two swallows visited me. They were exhausted, unable to use their claws to grip the deck or ropes. One sat on the side deck, the other in the cockpit. I picked up the one on the side deck and brought it into the shelter of the cockpit. My daily routine of emptying the bilge, trimming sails and talking to myself did not bother them.

Flying in the air were numerous tiny insects. When the birds had rested, they took to the air, diving and darting after the insects, and feeding on them. It looked like hard work. No wonder they were exhausted. When they left, I missed their company.

During the night I turned on the VHF radio. After ten hours' silence, I began to hear chatter. Suddenly a coastal station came through loud and clear. Valentia Radio off the Kerry coast gave the weather forecast. An anti-cyclone was centred over Ireland and would continue to drift east.

For several days progress was good. I was still heading north-east. My sun sights in between the spells of fog put me off the Irish coast near the Shannon estuary. I estimated that I was about 100 miles offshore, and still making a course towards Scotland.

Most of my food was exhausted except for the pasta and that had to be cooked in fresh water. There were two cups of water left, and three cans of peas which would yield some liquid. My tongue was thick and swallowing had become difficult. Thirst is a horrible feeling. I looked at the bottle of champagne Mark Schrader had given me. It was a liquid, but alcohol would dehydrate me very rapidly. Besides, I wanted to save it for the day I crossed the finishing line in Newport, even though it was a long time away.

On 8 September I saw a fishing boat pass. I radioed her, but to no avail. The water was as calm as a mirror, but my first opportunity to go alongside a vessel for water had been foiled. I was angry that no one had heard me. Later the fog cleared and I went below to sleep.

In the afternoon I was awakened by the sound of a propeller. I rushed on deck to see a thick blanket of fog again, but the engine could still be heard. The drone was close-by, but I could not pinpoint where. Then the fog became patchy and later cleared. I could see a fishing boat about two miles away. I got out my binoculars and read the name as *Girl* something.

I had a little fuel left, enough to motor for ten minutes. I lowered the two head sails and started the Yamaha engine, slowly motoring over with some help from the wind in the mainsail. About 150 meters away, a crew member on the deck spotted me waving. The vessel was trawling as I closed the gap. The crew rushed up to the wheelhouse and moments later a second head popped out. I waved frantically to ensure that they knew I wanted their attention. The vessel stopped. As I got within hailing distance, I heard someone say go to VHF channel 6.

On channel 6 I explained that I had lost my rudder and needed water. The captain of the *Girl Cleonia* told me to come alongside. I set up fenders and mooring lines and then motored in. The five crew took my lines and welcomed me aboard. It was my first physical contact with another human being since the Azores 27 days before and it felt good.

7

LAND AHOY

On the evening of the 4th of July, I sighted a yacht on the horizon, calling her up 'as the racing yacht on my western horizon with spectra sails'. She replied immediately, identifying herself as *Europa 93*. It was José Ugarte, a 63-year-old Spaniard.

From him I learnt who had finished and what records were smashed. In my class, Simon van Hagen on *Seatalk* had won, breaking his own record set four years before to finish in an astonishing feat of 17 days. He had a new boat built for the race, which was two feet bigger than *Stella-r*.

I was told that Irish entrant, Robin Deasy sailing *Spirit of Ireland,* had abandoned his trimaran in mid-Atlantic after hitting a floating obstacle. A ship bound for the Netherlands took him off after he activated his distress beacon. Several weeks later, the boat was seen afloat near the Azores Islands. Robin flew there and eventually with the help of the Portuguese Navy, salvaged his boat and returned with what was left to Ireland.

I continued to sail as fast as possible. Colin Chapman on *Deerhound*, whose position was reported daily on high frequency radio, and Francois Bourgeois in *DDGF* were not far ahead. This knowledge forced me to decide to go across the Nantucket shoals.

I arrived on the shoals at daybreak in light winds. Looking at the detailed chart, a passage was selected. Once committed, there would be no turning back. With five knots of wind, I could keep my boat moving, but when the tide turned against me, it was difficult. There were narrow channels with just enough water in which to stay afloat. Outside the channel, *Stella-r* would be aground. Navigation had to be precise; there was no room for error.

At times I made only half a knot through the water, but I was moving in the right direction. If the wind became any less, there would be no other option but to anchor and wait until the wind returned.

Tide often is stronger in the shallower channels. Where the water permitted, I crossed the sand bars to get into deeper channels and so minimise the tides. Occasionally on top of the sand bars I found different currents, and used them to my advantage. There were huge overfalls of cresting waves trying to swamp into the boat as currents reacted to each other, making progress very hard since as it shook the wind out of the sails, with *Stella-r* bobbing about. It was nerve-racking, but many miles towards Newport would be saved.

In the afternoon the breeze freshened and boat speed improved. Ten hours after arriving on the Nantucket shoals, I sighted Nantucket Island through the haze to starboard. It was now 70 miles to the finish. An hour later, I sailed into deeper water. The wind was on my beam. I piled on all the sail I could and filled the windward water ballast tank. It would take ten hours at an average of 6.6 knots to reach the finish.

Thick fog rolled in. I chose to helm instead of using my windvane, pushing the boat as hard as I dared. All my three Autohelm autopilots failed, as they did on several other boats. It would be a shame to be so close to the finish and to risk losing the mast over the side if the space frame broke. But *Deerhound* was close by and had to be beaten. It was a race and calculated risks had to be taken. The breeze freshened. My boat speed increased to 8 knots over the ground with the beginning of a favourable tide.

The fog was worrisome as the Brendon Tower, one point of the finish line, was close inshore, and the flashing buoy marking the other end was on the edge of a reef.

My excitement grew as the tidal flow increased, bringing the big moment of my life closer. Ten miles from the finish, *Stella-r* sailed out of the fog bank. I could see a bright light flash, and thought that it was the Brendon Tower, but its flashing frequency was incorrect. My heart leapt in fear that my navigation was wrong and that I had found some other light instead. I looked at the chart. The Brendon Tower could be visible from twenty miles. My position according to the Garmin GPS was correct. Then I looked at the land on the chart behind the tower and saw that the Beaver light was the flashing frequency I had noticed, close to the Brendon Tower. It was a weaker light, which confused me because I still could not see the Tower.

I returned to helming. Four miles from the Tower I saw it flash ever so faintly and, at 04:54 GMT, the bow of *Stella-r* crossed the finish line. I felt exhilarated. No chemical substance could create feelings of such accomplishment as I felt on that morning of 6 July. As a child, I had imagined being at the helm of a big ocean racing yacht, surfing down waves through the thick fog towards the Brendon Tower, feeling the cool wind in my damp hair. That dream had come true.

Shortly after finishing, a boat took *Stella-r* in tow. When we came into the harbour, past Fort Adams, a harbour patrol launch powered close by with her blue warning light flashing. Near the dock at which I was to berth, she turned on her blaring siren, bringing down fellow competitors and a small crowd of spectators. Several competitors in my class were already tied up on the dock. They had finished the previous evening, within eighteen hours of me. Forty-four boats had beaten me out of the fleet of 78 starters, and I was seventh in my class of nine. I had beaten *DDGF* and *Deerhound*.

I had not slept since leaving George's Bank. Exhaustion had caught up with me, but I opened the BOC champagne and telephoned Ireland and South Africa to share my joy, before falling asleep.

Over the days to come, boats slowly trickled in. There was always great excitement when another boat finished, and I felt sad that the race was almost over. There was an emptiness and I felt depressed. To occupy my mind, I looked at the repairs that needed doing. There were several. I was given only three days' free berthing, then had to go on to a mooring. Electricity was needed to carry out the repairs. I mentioned this to Steve Black, a competitor from Newport in the race.

Steve arranged for me to go to the Newport Yacht Club, and introduced me to several people, helped organise tools and materials, and gave me a lot of encouragement. Soon work was started.

Among several of the competitors left in Newport, I became good friends with a Dutchman, Henk Bezema, from L.J. Harry. His next campaign was to be the two-handed Round Britain and Ireland Race. He regarded the race as more challenging than the Transatlantic event and he encouraged me to enter.

In late July, news came in that a close friend had scuttled his boat 400 miles from the finish. Jack Gansell had been dismasted on *Amber 2*. He had tried to construct a jury mast, but in the seaway was unable to make progress. Thus he had activated his distress beacon. He still owed money on his boat and he had no insurance, but gave up trying to fulfil his dream.

The last man to finish was Mike Richie in *Jester*. He had taken 45 days to reach Newport. It was his twenty-first solo Atlantic crossing. He was met on the dock by a large press reception and many friends. He was asked what his best position on the race was, having done eight single-handed transatlantic races. His reply was last. The question was repeated, requesting his best finishing place.

'Last,' he replied. 'I am always last. When the going gets tough, I lower my sail and read, eat, sleep and drink. I'm in no hurry.'

In the 1988 race Mike had lost the original *Jester*. That boat had done every transatlantic race, the first two races under the command of Blondie Hasler, one of the founders of the race in 1958. A replica of the original boat was built, and Mike sailed again.

Mike and I were the last foreign competitors left in Newport. Dr Freddie Olofson who was chairman of the Rhode Island State Yachting Association, and the former mayor of Newport, was hosting a dinner to welcome Mike back to Newport. I was asked to ensure that I attend.

The dinner was at Christies restaurant. The entire top floor dining room was reserved for twenty guests. We were offered an elaborate menu, and I had one of the best meals eaten on that side of the Atlantic.

After dinner Dr Olofson rose. He produced a gold medal on a tricolour ribbon.

'This medal, the Medal of Honour,' he said, 'grants the bearer the Key to this city. We give only a few deserving people this honour. At seventy-five years of age, a young man has crossed the Atlantic for the twenty-first time single-handed, sailing in one of the smallest boats. On behalf of the Mayor, I present Mike Richie with this honour, the oldest man in sailing history to have crossed any ocean single-handed.'

There are only two international Halls of Fame — tennis and yachting. Mike Richie was one of a few men to have his piece of history made, detailed in the Yachting Hall of Fame in Fort Adams which overlooks Newport Harbour.

Dr Olofson continued. 'The second recipient came here from the furthest destination, and against the odds. He was unsponsored and holed thrice. But this young man has set an example of what courage, determination and dedication is, and has been a ambassador to both his native South Africa and his adopted country, Ireland.

'Most of all, he has been an ambassador to sailing, bring the messages of protecting our environment and using education to achieve goals. On behalf of the Mayor, I give Neal Petersen the Key to the City of Newport.'

My eyes swelled with tears of joy. I took minutes to compose myself. The ribbon was placed over my head with the gold medal hanging on my chest.

'This is the greatest honour I have ever received. On behalf of all the people who made this possible, I accept this honour,' I said proudly. 'I wish to thank this city for giving us such a wonderful finish, the Royal Western Yacht Club for starting the race, but most important, I want to thank my parents who encouraged me, the individuals in South Africa who had faith in my dream, and the Irish, especially those people of Galway who not only gave me hope, but who welcomed me into their homes and lives, to give me so much to realise this dream. Without these people, I would not be here. Thank you all.'

For years I dreamed of finishing the solo transatlantic race. I never expected any medals. So much had changed from the previous year when I had been in the Atlantic with no drinking water. I had no idea how my life would change after meeting the *Girl Cleonia*.

***

The first thing the skipper, Tony Flaherty from the Aran Islands at the entrance to Galway Bay, did when he heard that I had been at sea for 27 days, was to ask one of his crew to cook me a steak. The first thing I wanted was to drink a glass of milk, but it felt good to eat a satisfying meal.

Explaining to Tony how I had sailed my boat 1,100 miles to meet him, I babbled on about the gales and being scared of loosing my mental sanity, and that it was my dream to do the solo transatlantic race. I asked whether they had any spare petrol aboard and a chart of the coast that I could borrow. They had neither, but were able to fill all my water jugs. I could survive for another month at sea until I safely made land.

I was not quite ready to cast off. It was calm and I was able to remain alongside. They had resumed trawling in the direction of Galway Bay, 70 miles away. Tony had to return to the wheelhouse to ensure that they were still on course. I stayed in the saloon drinking milk and talking to his crew. Not having had company for a month, I did a lot of talking! When Tony came down, he said he had reported my position to the coastal station. Since he was able to reach a coastal station, I requested whether I could use his radio to call home.

My family would have been extremely worried about me because I was two weeks overdue. My radio did not have the range to contact a coastal station. I explained my detailed situation to my mother, telling her not to worry because I now had enough water and could get some basic provisions off the fishing boat to survive. I asked her to try to contact a friend at Manex Marine in Cape Town to see if he could talk to a few people about trying to raise some sponsorship so that I could have the funds to repair my boat and still make the start of the transatlantic race.

This conversation was overheard by a naval vessel on patrol. Tony Flaherty had already informed the coastal authority of my situation. After overhearing my conversation, and a report was made to the Marine Rescue co-ordinator at Shannon, who called me up on the *Girl Cleonia* to find out my intentions. I explained that I was self-sufficient, having sailed half-way across the Atlantic with no rudder, and would in time make a safe port. This was not good enough for them. They did not want a disabled vessel so close to their shores. At that moment the weather might have been fine, but there was no telling if, days later, when I was closer to the coast, gales might blow and I was in danger of going aground. Then they would have to launch a full-scale search and rescue for me, at great difficulty and possible risk.

They offered to send out the lifeboat from the Aran Islands. I explained that I would be all right and did not have the funds to pay for a tow. They argued that, even though I was an experienced sailor and might be able to reach port safely, the risk was too great, their reputation was at stake, and, if things went wrong, the cost of rescuing me would be exorbitant.

At that point a second party came onto the frequency identifying itself as the naval vessel, the *LE Orla*. Her captain told Shannon Rescue Control that they were less than three hours steaming away and would be willing to go to my assistance, which would not tie up the lifeboat.

I remained alongside the *Girl Cleonia* for another hour. The breeze had picked up and a slight chop was on the water. Tony wanted to lift his trawl. It would be easier for him without a yacht alongside. I was cast adrift, but nearly with a mishap. My stern mooring line was in the water as I retrieved the bowline. It got sucked under the trawler's stern. One of crew spotted the potential problem and shouted at the wheelhouse to disengage the engine, while I retrieved the line.

Once the trawl had been lifted, the fishing boat returned to me. I had begun setting up the towing line, taking ropes around the mast, cleats and winches to distribute the towing loads over the deck. I past the *Girl Cleonia* a shorter tow line and asked that she stay below five knots. As she began towing me, the *LE Orla* appeared on the horizon. *Girl Cleonia* started towing me towards her, with the *Stella-r* broaching severely. The speed of the tow had to be reduced to three knots.

Soon the *Girl Cleonia* cast me off and the *Orla* took over. I passed them my heavy anchor rope. The line was secured, and the towing began. Once we got to over three knots, I again started to broach in her wake. The captain noticed this and stopped. He put a searider inflatable boat in the water containing his navigating officer, his bosun and two deckhands.

Using the ship's mooring lines over the *Stella-r's* stern, we solved the problem. The tow was resumed. Soon we were up to ten knots with no difficulty and with no risk of broaching. The navigating officer took down details of my nationality and my vessel's port of registration, last port of call and future plans. Thereafter he and one deckhand returned to the *LE Orla*, leaving the bosun and the other deckhand on board the *Stella-r* to keep me company and to be at the ready if we had further trouble with the tow during the night.

Once the boat had settled down, I was invited aboard the *LE Orla* to meet the captain and have a shower. I was transferred without the boats being slowed down. Once aboard, I was shown to a cabin and the showers. Having a hot shower was bliss. For weeks I had been conserving water, and now suddenly I had plenty of water to dance under. Then I was shown to the bridge and was introduced to Lieutenant Commander Mark Mellett. We spoke about my voyage and aspirations. I thanked him for taking the trouble to go out of his way to escort me. He offered me a bunk aboard his ship, but I felt it would be improper of me to abandon my boat.

When I returned to the *Stella-r*, I brought some refreshments for the two sailors. We settled down for the night, checking the tow every so often to ensure that we would not damage the deck or chaff the rope. During the night the wind freshened from the north-west for several hours. The sea became lumpy, but it did not affect the tow.

Early the following morning we were off Galway city, but could not see it because the fog had closed in. The tow was slipped as the *LE Orla* dropped anchor. We motored alongside her to await the tide and the opening of the lock gate. Two hours before high water, the lock opened and the pilot went aboard the naval vessel. I was given additional fuel and motored as quickly as possible after them, fearing that I might lose sight of the *LE Orla* in the fog.

Once in the harbour, the searider helped me tie up. I briefly tidied the boat before going to breakfast with the officers of the *LE Orla* in their wardroom. When I returned to the *Stella-r*, there was a gentleman waiting on the dock for me. He introduced himself as Brian Lynch, a fellow yachtsman who had been in the Aran Islands over the weekend and had overheard the communications between the vessels and coastal station. He had kindly come down to see if there was anything he could do to help me. I asked him to drop me at a vegetable shop. I had not eaten any fresh fruit or vegetables for four weeks and wanted to get some. When I took out my wallet at the checkout, Brian would hear none of it. We took the supplies onboard, and then went to the Customs and Excise. Before departing Brian asked if there was anything else he could do for me. I said that I would be interested in meeting members of the press.

It took a while to find the officials that dealt with shipping. An officer in plain clothes with a big beard dealt with me. When my story was told, everyone became interested. They wanted to know how I had coped with the difficulties, and for such a prolonged period of isolation, especially without female company! I was given coffee. An hour later, two of the officers asked to see the boat, explaining that they would like to have a look at my medical kit.

We walked down. As we approached the boat, I noticed an array of people on the dockside. They were from the national television station, radio and the newspapers. Customs asked them to wait until the boat had been officially cleared in. The two officers came aboard and looked around while I got out my medical kit. Peter Clinton went through my medical supplies, asking me to identify certain drugs and what they were for. After a while they were satisfied and left.

My attention now turned to the media. Among them was a distinguished-looking grey-haired gentleman in his early forties with glasses. He knew everybody. Then a face appeared beside him, one that I knew. It was none other than Enda O'Coineen talking to Jim Fahy. I had met Enda at the BOC press conference in London two years before. He had planned to enter the 1990-91 BOC, but unfortunately was first late for the start, and then, on the second day out, he collided with a fishing vessel and was dismasted.

Enda introduced me to Jim and a few other journalists who were curious to know how a black South African kid could have a boat, and sail seven thousand miles to Ireland unsponsored. I explained that I had been poorly supported by big businesses in South Africa, and was still in search of a sponsor.

'If one has a dream and believes fully in it and oneself,' I said, 'with determination and dedication it can be achieved. I want to finish the race and set an example for all people that dreams can be realised. I might be young, and from a working-class background where I have no human rights in South Africa, but I will get to the starting line, and finish.'

That interview went out that evening on the national television news. I watched it aboard the *LE Orla* with her captain. In the days to follow, journalists from national and international newspapers, and local radio contacted me. Most ran the story of the young solo sailor rescued off the Irish coast. I was annoyed at the word 'rescued', but it was what gripped the media and even though no rescue had taken place, it made news.

The following day one of the customs officer's returned to the boat. He wanted to have another look again at the medical kit. It was still where I had left it. With the increase in drugs on Irish streets, the customs were worried that small quantities were being smuggled in by yacht. After more questions, he stamped my passport and left.

Enda arrived, inviting me to lunch with a few sailors. It was there that I met John Killeen, who was to become one of my best friends and an enthusiast of my project.

Numerous people had come down to look at me after seeing my face in the papers and on television. That evening I had just finished supper when another car pulled up and a man called down from the jetty. He was very interested in how the boat had been built. I invited Kevin Hallinan aboard, showing him the damage and my accommodation. He was amazed at how spartan the interior was.

As he was leaving, he asked how I liked the local beer. I said that I had not tried the Guinness, and had not been to the pub. I am a tee-totaller, but was interested in seeing an Irish pub. He took it upon himself to introduce me to a few pubs. Eventually, towards late evening we ended up in a pub called Naughtons, very close to the boat.

Kevin had to go home to his wife but I stayed on. The traditional music was great. I had never heard Irish music before. It was here Malcolm Goodbody introduced himself to me, his friends called him Paddy. I stayed talking to Paddy and it turned out that he had been sailing in Portugal the previous year, and was very keen on canoeing and caving. We had an interesting evening before I wandered back to the boat. Paddy gave me his office number, saying that I was to call him the following day to arrange lunch and that I could go to his home to do my laundry.

We skipped lunch because he was very busy at his office, but he did told me how to find his home. He gave me a front door key and said that any time I wanted a warm dry bed, there was a spare one there. What he did not know was that my boat was very damp and that I would frequently need that spare bed. It was the beginning of a special friendship that was to take us caving and kayaking in western Ireland

Kevin returned that evening to see if I wanted to go to the local sailing club. There was a Wednesday evening race, and John Killeen invited me aboard his former Admiral's Cup forty-footer, *Mayhem*. One of the crew was

Jim Fahy. We had a good race. I trimmed the mainsail, which became my job on board.

The winter of 1991 turned into a very busy one. I needed help to fix the boat, and set out to look for someone who knew a lot about fibreglass. I asked the harbourmaster, Frank Sheridan, who recommended Eugene Waters of Fibre Glass Engineers. Over the phone, Eugene asked Frank if I had a lot of money. Frank said there was none. Eugene came down that afternoon. After seeing what had to be done, he recommended that I ask John Killeen if I could get *Stella-r* into his shed, next door to his place. His suggestion was that I do as much as I could myself, and when stuck, he would help in his free time.

The customs officer, Peter Clinton invited me out to the pub on Friday evenings. The pub in Ireland is the centre of single life, not because of the drinking, but the social get-together and the music. It was in one of the pubs that a university student came up to me. We chatted and days later she visited me at the boat.

The student invited me to a lecture by Bishop Eamonn Casey. I had heard of this man in my travels, and was keen to meet him. He was chairing a discussion entitled, 'Ireland as a Third World Country.' After his lecture, I went up to speak to him. He had seen me on television. As we were chatting, a young lady came up and the Bishop introduced me as a famous South African sailor. Rosie Coyne and I got talking, then I met her friend Mary. Several days later, the girls invited me to their home to dinner.

John and Enda were involved in a youth sail training vessel, the *Pride of Galway*, 100-foot gaff-rigged ketch. For several days they were around a lot until Enda had to drive back to Dublin. I still saw John, since I had been invited to race with him and Jim again. They had planned to take *Mayhem* to County Cork for the October League racing, held Sunday morning for the month. It began three weeks later. I was asked to help deliver the boat the following weekend.

After three weeks of gales, I got *Mayhem* down to Crosshaven on the weekend of the first race. The following Saturday, at the Galway Bay Sailing Club, was the end of season 'lift out' of all the boats. John had offered me space in his shed and would trailer the boat there. It had been arranged with the commodore of the club, David Baines, to lift *Stella-r* with the club boats, but the person

Keel torn out of hull in Galway.
Photoghapher: R.M Goodbody

responsible for supervising the lift out was not informed until I arrived with the boat. I had to come alongside near the top of the tide. There was pandemonium getting the boats out. Everybody wanted to be lifted immediately, instead of the smaller boats first and the bigger boats near the top of the tide, followed by smaller boats later again.

I was told to wait until the member's boats had been lifted. *Stella-r* went aground as the tide began falling. She started to settle backwards because there was no rudder to rest on. In the late afternoon there were only five boats left to lift. I went aboard to find more frames broken in the stern area and the hull inverting. She had to be propped or the keel would come through the hull. It was agreed to lift the boat next.

Once in the slings suspended by the crane, the keel had to be taken off. I unscrewed the bolts, except for one that was turning on itself. There was no light in the boat, so I could not see properly. In the collision with the solid object, the leading keel bolt sheared and was turning on itself within the keel. I needed time to sort it out, but outside there was a rush to free up the crane. There was no cradle for me to sit in, so it was decided to put me back against the wall until the other boats were out of the water. Unfortunately, when the slings were slackened off, *Stella-r* wanted to sit outward. She was turned around having slid, but would not rest. Someone decided to put her on the hard, on her side. John and I strongly objected to this, but our pleas were brushed aside.

As the boat was put down at an angle, I heard the splintering of wood. With every millimetre lowered by the crane, my boat began to crumple. The crane driver lifted the boat at my screams, but it was too late. The keel was pushed to one side and the hull splintered. She had to be lowered and the keel torn out of the boat. My heart sank. My home, my transport and my ocean dreams had been ruined. I walked away. John took me to Paddy's home where I cried myself to sleep.

The next day I went down to see what was to be done. It was depressing. *Stella-r* sat upon her keel, with twisted and mangled wood projecting from beneath the hull. The damage appeared to be so bad, I feared that she would never sail again. John got somebody down to cut the offending bolt. Three boats had to be lifted on the Sunday. John had to go to Crosshaven to race, but arranged for a sailing friend of his to help me.

We lifted *Stella-r*. Since the hull was splintered, the keel came off easily. John's friend and a few people standing around helped get *Stella-r* onto the trailer and propped. The keel would be left for another time. I had to pay the club £80 for the use of the crane, double the cost for members.

The following day John took off work to trailer the boat to the shed. We got it in, and used a fork lift to put it up on drums. It was sad to see my pride and joy with her belly torn out.

8

ISLANDS OF FRIENDS

It was hot and clammy. The harbourmaster towed *Stella-r* to the Newport Yacht Club, where during the week while the marina was quiet, I could carry out repairs. Roger Martin, a former South African who had designed several BOC yachts, came over and offered his expert advise. He lent me a bicycle to get around Rhode Island.

It was not pleasant working with fibre glass in the summer heat. The bow area, where she had been repaired in Baltimore, Co. Cork at the beginning of the race, neededadditional support. The inside of the hull had to be laminated with fibre glass mat to reduce flexing in the hull and give it rigidity. Between the Baltimore repair and main bulkhead, on both port and starboard side, a perpendicular stringer to the hull had to be laminated so that I could attach a tie rod from beneath the chain plates to the hull to secure the rigging. This was to replace the aluminium space frame because the weld had sheared.

***

Before the race in Ireland, with the help of nearly forty people, I rebuilt *Stella-r* during the winter of 1991. After the keel had been torn out of the hull in the sailing club in Galway, John Killeen trailered the *Stella-r* to his shed in Oranmore, nine kilometres outside the city and beside Cold Chon, the bitumen manufacturing company of which John was managing director. I moved in to Paddy's home and, in the mornings, drove out to the shed with John.

It was awful to see *Stella-r* with a huge splintered gapping hole in the bottom. She looked unsalvagable, but I was going to try to do repairs. Everything on the interior had to be removed and stored. Fortunately, the shed was huge, some sixty foot wide by a hundred and fifty foot long.

I asked John if he had a jigsaw I could borrow. His words were: 'Leave it with me.' I did. The following morning a truck containing some tools arrived. A bench planer, an industrial band saw, a lathe and a huge circular saw were offloaded, along with other tools. John had sent over enough tools to build a new yacht.

I began cutting away the splintered wood. Eugene Waters showed me how to peel back the laminated wood until I reached undamaged wood, about 30 cm from the hole. It was painstaking work. I cursed a lot, because if care and patience had been taken when lifting out the boat, damage to the hull could have been avoided. I admit that the keel could easily have come off after the stringer had broken, but strengthening work on the inside of the hull had been planned.

My biggest nightmare was how I was going to fund the major repairs. No company would sponsor a yacht with a gapping hole in the bottom, with no assurance that it would ever float again, let alone race safely across the Atlantic. Besides, when the yacht had been launched, no one saw the potential in South Africa to sponsor me.

Brian Lynch believed that he knew of such a company. He established a contact with Colm DeBarra, who put him in contact with the public relations manager, Gus Barrett, before he got my hopes up that DeBeers Industrial Diamonds of Shannon would help me. Various press clippings were sent to them, before they decided to throw me a lifeline. The company was not interested in publicity or the gains that sponsorship brought. They just wanted to be part of my challenge. I was invited to their plant and shown around before being given a cheque for a sizeable amount. Without their money, I would not have sailed the *Stella-r* again. Thank you for your generosity.

Essential materials were bought. Work began fulltime on the boat, seven days a week. When John was out of town on business, I stayed aboard *Stella-r* in the shed. Often I got into some job that had to be finished, and would not leave. Once the damaged wood had been cleared away and solid wood was reached, I began slowly to stitch the hole shut using mahogany veneers and epoxy. It took time. On the inside, from beneath each ballast tank, I laminated layer upon layer of fibre glass to strengthen the hull. On the outside I also laminated several layers of fibre glass, creating a sandwich construction, before filling in the small irregularities with epoxy fillers. Sanding the hull back to a uniform shape was frustrating work.

I felt that the strength of the wood and fibreglass was not enough. The weight of the keel and mast had to be distributed over a greater area. John and I spent many hours looking at the completed work, eventually deciding that a space frame was need. He knew just the man to help me. Working in another of John's companies was Peter McDonagh, an aluminium welder.

John, Peter and I were below in the saloon looking at the hull. I said to them that we needed to run a beam down the middle of the hull, with limbs going to port and starboard.

'Stop!' Peter exclaimed. 'I don't sail. It is left and right, back and front.'

That was how Peter was introduced to sailing. He became a good, reliable crew. Two lengths of aluminium box section were ordered. He put in weeks of late nights cutting and welding the box until it fitted in the boat. It was slow work but Peter was meticulous.

While Peter worked on the space frame, I ordered a new bearing system for the rudder and a solid aluminium 40mm thick rod from which to make the rudder stock. This was tapered and had various attachments welded onto it so that the stock would not turn inside the rudder blade. Foam was shaped and bonded to the rudder, then laminated with fibreglass. Eugene helped me, getting the finished shape right on both sides. Eventually the rudder was complete, light enough for one person to carry, and slightly buoyant.

I was invited to give a lecture to the Castle Park Foróige club. Foroige is the National Youth Development Council. There are more than 500 clubs throughout Ireland. Later the next month, it was arranged for the club to visit the boat one evening in the shed, where the club leader, Dennis Barrett, and a youth leader brought them out. On the next weekend, Michael Hern, Liam and Jonathan Curan, Wesley O'Shaughnessy, Dave Heaney and Pascal Flaherty from Castle Park walked nine kilometres in the rain to share in my dream. They were all fourteen or fifteen. Castle Park is a council housing estate in Galway. Many people who live there are unemployed. In that community poverty and hardship can easily be found.

When the six boys arrived at my boat, they were drenched. I did not know whether to send them back, or set them to work. They had come to help and would have been very disappointed if there was nothing to do. They helped scrub the deck, preparing it for painting, sanded the hull ready for the spraying and generally tidied up the shed. Peter Clinton and his girlfriend came out often to help on Saturdays, giving the boys a lift home. Slowly the boat began taking shape.

Christmas came and went. Jim Fahy was down at the boat with a film crew. I had only taken time off to deliver *Mayhem* back to Galway after the October League, and to lecture in schools around the city. My weekly lectures were on my travels and experiences underwater, stressing the environmental issues regarding our planet about which I felt strongly.

After the programme was aired, I was in Dublin's Grafton Street, dodging the Christmas crowds, when a student who had seen me on television tapped me on my shoulder. He said that he was able to identify with my challenge, and wished to contribute something. He put his hand in his pocket and took out all the coins he had. Before

I could respond, he vanished into the crowd. He had given me £3.20.

Instead of cooking my own turkey, Rosie Coyne invited me home to her parent's place. Thereafter we were off to London for the Boat Show.

In the Autumn of 1991 I met a woman in a pub in Galway, who worked for the BBC. Lizzie Jackson interviewed me for a British radio programme, 'Does He Take Sugar'. She took a personal interest in my project, helping in my quest for sponsorship and sending out press releases. In London, Rosie and I stayed with her.

The Boat Show was hectic. As a result of Lizzie's hard work, I was interviewed by The London *Times*. At the show I met two of the directors from Central Boating whom I knew from Cape Town. They had given me a discount when I was buying gear to build my boat and now introduced me to Mark Luffingham of Robertson Stowe Marine, who sponsored me with an array of electronics. Mark in turn introduced me to Clive Bartlett of WSA, a marketing house for Garmin GPS and VC Systems anti-fouling. I came away with the loan of a GPS and anti-fouling. On the Monitor Windvane stand, I met Hans Burwell whom Mark Schrader had introduced me to at the Long Beach Boat Show in California. He sold me a windvane, the best self-steering gear that I have.

I was looking longingly at foul weather gear on the Henri Lloyd stand, when the managing director noticed my t-shirt. It had 'Protect our Sealife' written across the front, with OSTAR 92 and my name in small letters on the breast. He asked me about it. I explained that I was preparing to do the solo crossing and was a keen environmentalist. He liked my project, and sponsored me with foul weather gear.

The help I received at the Boat Show was invaluable. (Thank you to all my sponsors and supporters.) When I returned to Ireland, I appeared on one of the most popular television chat shows, *Kenny Live*, and was interviewed by

Pat Kenny. It was an interesting live programme, the first time I appeared live on television. I was very nervous, but Pat was a good interviewer.

In February 1992, I was shocked to get a phone call from the Gardai, the Irish police. When I had arrived in Ireland six months before, I was put under the impression that when Customs cleared me, they also dealt with the immigration because they stamped my passport and told me that all formalities were complete and to enjoy my stay. The Garda responsible for immigration at the local Garda station in Galway, read an article about my plans in a local newspaper. When he read that I was living in the city and had my boat at Cold Chon, he checked his file. Nowhere on their records was a file of my arrival in the country. He contacted me through the Cold Chon office, arranging an appointment for me to see him. On my way to him, I coincidentally met the journalist who had written the article about me that had brought my presence to the attention of the Garda officer. In a passing comment, I made the mistake of telling him where I was going.

It was a formality. The Garda wanted his paperwork in order, requiring passport photos, a bank statement and an assurance that I was not working in the country. We chatted about my career at sea, and he seemed genuinely interested. I got an official stamp in my passport until end of June, though I only planned to remain until mid-May.

Several days later, an article appeared in The Connacht Tribune newspaper and the next day in a national newspaper, that the country had labelled me as an illegal alien and had threatened me with deportation. It was incorrect because I had no problem with the Aliens office. It did created an embarrassing situation the next time I met the Garda. I wondered if the articles had any bearing on future relations with that department because when I returned to the country in September, I had to reapply and have had difficulty obtaining temporary residence.

As if that was not enough, a week later The Connacht Tribune ran a front page news item that I had started a fire on my boat, and that the local fire brigade had been called out. What really happened was that Eugene was repairing my damaged keel. Michael O' Ceallaigh with the help of Steelforms, made a new keel spacer box to deepen the keel, embedding new bolts in it.

After Michael had completed the welding, the keel was taken next door to Fibre Glass Engineering where I worked on it under Eugene's supervision. One morning the keel was dragged outside his workshop to create space for a large job. I was next door on *Stella-r* when I heard him shout for me to hurry quickly. I ran out to see smoke rising from his workshop. By the time I got to the entrance, thick black noxious smoke were coming out of a door beyond which numerous barrels of chemicals were stored.

I ran in thinking that Eugene had passed out. I could hear the flames roaring. Several times I called his name, getting no response. Soon I heard him calling me outside.

Eugene told me to summon the fire brigade, while he filled buckets with sand to dump on the flames and turned on the hose to dampen down the floor. Eugene pulled out his new spraygun and a twenty litre drum of resin. Someone arrived with a chemical fire extinguisher. In the factory were several, but I did not know where to find them. This person was trying to spray the chemicals from the door, not near the flames. I grabbed the fire extinguisher and soon the flames were smothered.

When the fire brigade arrived twenty minutes later, only smoke was pouring out of the factory. They went through to ensure that nothing was burning, spraying more chemicals on what was smouldering. One fireman commented that there were two black men running around who had put out the fire. One had an Irish accent. From then on Eugene called me Sunshine and was grateful for my help.

From time to time I delivered yachts for a fee. Michael Craughwell, to whom I had given some navigation classes, asked me to deliver a boat to Galway from the Hamble river near Southampton at the south coast of England. He had bought it second hand, but not having the expertise, wanted an experienced skipper.

It was a disastrous job. We were due to fly from Dublin to Heathrow. The flight was delayed for four hours because of fog. Michael's wife had cooked us a gorgeous curry to be eaten at sea. This saved my crew having to cook on a rolling craft. Passing through Heathrow Airport, my crew — Tim Gunning who I met through sailing on the *Pride of Galway*, and Mike's son Laurel were stopped. A policeman wanted to see what was in the pot. The whiff of curry sent him reeling. In London, we were in a tremendous hurry, and went to the wrong station for the train to Southampton. We had to lug our heavy bags back across London on the tube.

While Mike got the tickets, we loaded our gear onto the train. As Mike stepped onto the platform, the train pulled out, leaving him behind with all the tickets! Eventually he caught up with us on the next train. I had to explain the situation to the ticket collector on the train, who found it very amusing.

When we arrived at Hamble Point Marina, the boat, which was supposed to be all set, was not even launched and was far from ready to sail. I had suggested to Mike to buy a Garmin handheld GPS, an electronic navigation aid, since it was good and needed no installation. Instead he bought something else because it was slightly cheaper, but it had to be installed by someone he had contracted to work on the boat. This installation was done at the eleventh hour, and it did not work correctly.

Finally we sailed. The GPS gave constant trouble. Off Plymouth the Autohelm autopilot gave trouble and needed repair. I decided to call in at Queen Anne's Battery Marina to have the electronics looked at. Three miles from the marina, as we were motoring in, we got a blocked fuel line. We arrived with the help of a friendly fisherman who gave us a tow.

We arrived on a Sunday, and were forced to stay overnight. The following day, after Mike had spent a lot of money, we sailed into not so pleasant conditions. The boat pounded into the chop in the English Channel, whipped up by twenty knot winds. Mike was seasick and could not face another two hundred miles. He begged me to put into Falmouth.

Mike and Laurel left the boat in Falmouth. Tim and I continued across the Celtic Sea in moderate conditions. Off Valentia Island, the batteries went flat and we could not start the engine. I radioed through to Shannon later in the afternoon, trying to let Mike know of the situation aboard. He could not be reached, so I asked Shannon Radio to relay to him that I was having battery problems, but we were alright and would call him at midnight when we were at the head of Galway Bay. I informed them that I was shutting down the radio and could not be contactable until approximately midnight. They asked me for my position, which was three miles off Loop Head lighthouse.

The GPS stopped working in the Celtic Sea. This did not bother me, because I had done numerous deliveries along the west coast and knew it very well. I could almost navigate it by looking at the coastline. Using a hand-bearing compass and a radio direction finder which I always carry with me on deliveries, I could navigate independently of the sail boat's instruments, and in fog.

The weather had been fresh since leaving Land's End and we were making good progress. The sea was rough and confused in the force seven to eight wind strength, forcing us to helm. We surfed off waves with two reefs in the mainsail and a small headsail.

About 21:00 we noticed a helicopter flying in the area. We did not pay much attention to it, because I was busy with the navigation and Tim was helming to my courses.

We had entered the South Sound between the Aran Islands and the Clare coast at the head of Galway Bay. An hour later, reaching along the coast in flat water at quite a speed and two hours ahead of schedule, I called up Shannon radio to ring Mike with our estimated time of arrive of 01:00, to learn that there was a red alert.

The chopper had been searching for us. Since we had not turned on the radio all afternoon, we did not hear the notice to shipping to keep a look-out for us, after Shannon Radio could not raise us. At sunset the Aran Island lifeboat had been launched, and two hours later the helicopter. Their searching had been in the wrong place. They expected me to give the coast a wide berth. Instead, I went close inshore to get a stronger tide.

When the chopper heard our transmission, they flew close to us, putting a bright searchlight on our sails. Half an hour later, the lifeboat came up our stern, wanting to take us in tow. I refused because we were not disabled, and in no trouble.

I thanked them for their concern, telling them all was well and that they could go home. It was cold, with rain showers lashing down. The chopper returned to base, but the lifeboat insisted on standing by until we were safely alongside in the harbour.

My plan was to anchor in the river close to the wall, then gradually to ease the anchor line until we were docked. With the lifeboat at hand, I decided that it would be easier going alongside her to let the lifeboat manoeuvre us beside the harbour wall. This did cause some damage to the boat because the bay was very choppy. It was minor damage with a bent stantion, damaging the deck slightly. Eugene was able to repair it easily.

When I got ashore, I wanted to know what all the fuss was about and who had called out the lifeboat. I learnt that Mike had panicked when he got the message, remembering all the earlier troubles. As a nervous and inexperienced owner, he shared his worries with Shannon

Marine Rescue Centre. Later he contacted John Killeen, telling him the situation and what he had done. John told him that he was worrying unnecessarily and contacted Shannon to inform them that I was an experienced sailor who knew the west coast and normally sailed a much bigger boat single-handedly without an engine. He suggested that they wait until the next day, but they refused to listen.

What infuriated me was that I had all the safety gear aboard which included new flares and a brand new distress beacon which I had shown to Mike.

This incident I managed to keep away from the media, who may have blown it out of proportion. Several people who heard of the incident from Mike, gave me a hard time about it, saying that I should not go onto the water because I was costing the taxpayer a fortune. This was unfair. If Mike had had more faith in my abilities, no one would have been inconvenienced. I gladly went back to work on my own boat.

In early March I was a guest speaker at a symposium at a hotel in Galway on adventure. Four guest speakers and myself were invited to give an account of our adventures. Jammie Young spoke of his trips which had taken him around Cape Horn and later to Guinea-Bissau, West Africa in canoes. The Portumna farmer, Robin Deacy, related humorously how he went to the UK to buy farming machinery and returned instead with a 60-foot trimaran. Overcoming his seasickness, Robin competed in the solo Transatlantic race in *Spirit of Ireland*. Then there were two engineers who had kayaked down rivers from the Arctic Circle to the Hudson Bay.

At that symposium I was introduced to a very pretty girl, Gwen Wilkinson. I could not resist asking her out that very evening to a dinner dance connected with the symposium. Sadly she stood me up.

Finally in late March the big day arrived. The boat had been spray-painted, and the deck had been painted grey instead of puke green. Stevin Durkin who ran Municipal Equipment Company made up a logo. This along with the decals of the name and slogan, *Stella-r, Protect our Sealife,* was done in reflective vinyl.

John personally drilled the keel bolt holes to ensure that it was done perfectly. *Stella-r* was lowered onto the trailer and towed out. She was taken to the Claddagh Basin, a historic part of old Galway where the traditional hooker boats traded between Ireland and Spain in the sixteenth century. Pete had the job of transporting the modified keel. The trailer was not strong enough and ended up at the roadside with a punctured tyre. Finally he brought the keel.

A crowd gathered round as we set the hull upon the keel. John had drilled the holes so precisely, that all the bolts matched the holes. The diameter of the holes was one millimetre greater than the bolts. Using a broken sleeper, we banged from the inside until the first nuts could be screwed on, then lifted the boat and released the brake on the crane to bounce the keel on the ground, forcing in the bolts. Eventually a large spanner was used to tighten it and *Stella-r* was launched.

My pride had been restored. It had taken a lot of neck to ask strangers for help, but they gave of their skills so willingly and became my friends. They did not have to help a newcomer, who was not even Irish and who could not repay them. When a man or woman rises high, people will toast them; but when an individual is at the bottom, it is often the nature of begrudgers to cast stones into the boat to sink it as quickly as possible. The people of Galway freely gave what they could to help me.

In April I had fitted the Monitor windvane, tightened the rig and tidied up the boat. I wanted a proper launching ceremony. The Mayor of Galway, Dr Michael Leahy, was asked officially to launch the *Stella-r*.

Eugene took me to meet a friend of his, Pete Green a Murphy's Brewery representative. Through Pete,

Murphy's gave me two kegs of beer for the occasion, and Eugene presented me with the launching bottle. Instead of the standard champagne, we had decided to use a traditional Irish drink, Murphy's stout.

It was a perfect sunny Sunday afternoon. A crowd of friends and spectators gathered at the basin. On the deck of *Stella-r* a guitarist strummed and sang sea shanties, while a poet gave us the privilege of hearing his own inspirational works. At 16:00 the roar of a helicopter was heard coming up the river, flying low as the RTE's cameraman began filming. Marcus Casey, a pilot who lived in the house with Paddy and me, had arranged with a friend of his, Ray McGrogan, owner of Helifly and a two seater-chopper for executive charter and flying lessons, to bring the Mayor in by air. It was a great day.

Soon we were ready to start sailing. The first sail of the season was costly. Since the Monitor windvane was on the stern, the outboard engine could not be tilted out of the water. I found the boat to be going significantly faster than before in the same wind strength. We beat into the bay, then gybed around and started back. The speed increased drastically, pivoting the 30 horse power outboard off the bracket; in my last-minute preparations and excitement, I had forgotten to tie it on. The ocean placed its hand aboard and grabbed the engine which I had planned to sell, so that I could pay the entry fee to the race.

I borrowed another engine off John. One weekend six of us planned to go to the Aran Islands. We departed early in the afternoon, sailing into rough weather. It was wet and miserable as we tried to beat our way out of the bay. Two persons aboard were very seasick, to the point that seven miles from the Islands, in the midst of a squall, I decided to turn back.

We returned pleasantly with staysail only. Our arrival at the harbour was before the tidal lock gates had opened. I struggled to get the outboard engine started and gave up. We sailed to 100m from the harbour and dropped anchor for an hour. Some heavy gusts howled through the rigging. A cargo boat came up the channel, and just at a crucial moment as the boat prepared to berth, my anchor broke fee. We dragged onto a collision path with them. The vessel tried to go astern, but we drifted on to her. My crew did a good job fending us off, getting *Stella-r* away with little damage. With some help from the cargo boat, we went alongside the pier safely.

A nightmare that still needed resolving was the balance of £500 for the entry fee to the Transatlantic race. I had approached various sailing bodies in South Africa to assist, but none was willing. I telephone John Joseph in Cape Town explaining my difficulty, which he discussed with Graham Lizamore. Together they contacted Hollard Insurance company, who kindly paid the entry fee. (Thank you to Rod Joubert who was the manager who helped, John and Graham.)

We had several memorable sails in Galway Bay. One lovely Sunday afternoon, Jim Fahy, eight friends and I went out for a few hours. We sailed back to the harbour, taking down the sails early in the fresh breeze, and were comfortably motoring in when the engine spluttered and stopped. I could not get it started before we had drifted onto the rocks on a falling tide. We managed to get a tow off quick enough, but I had had my fill of engines.

One final item of gear I still needed was an emergency distress beacon that operated on satellite frequencies. I did not have the funds to buy one, but I planned to rent one in England. Brian Lynch had often asked me about it, claiming that it was an essential safety item. Brian introduced me to a friend, Ronnie Robins, who had expressed an interest in my project. Ronnie, a Barrister from Dublin, offered to buy me one. Through that warm gesture, Ronnie became another close personal friend.

Preparations were made to leave Galway. Provisions were taken aboard, a farewell party arranged and the *Pride of Galway* was on its way to bid me farewell. The week before the arranged departure date, I arrived at the boat to find a sprig of heather, beautifully wrapped and placed in the cockpit, to bring me good luck, a short note with a poem:

> *Dark man*
> *with Gypsy locks*
> *and vagabond breath,*
> *pirate of hearts,*
> *set me as your figurehead*
> *and I shall scan the seas for you.*
>
> *Dark man*
> *with beady gull-like eyes,*
> *your gaze a slippery fish to hold,*
> *stare past and beyond out to sea*
> *a glimpse of merman*
> *scaling dreams.*

The handwriting was atrocious. It took the help of three friends to decipher the romantic words, but we could not read the signature. I did not have a clue from whom it was, except that it radiated a woman's tenderness. A year later I found out.

9

SOLO AGAIN

Every entrant who reached Newport was put up by a host family. I was fortunate to have two: Dianne, who ran an inn, and Ginny Long, who worked for the American Yachting Association. I was never without company.

In Newport sailing club, I made progress with my repairs. The commodore and vice commodore did everything they could to make my stay comfortable. They told me about their local solo race and several people encouraged me to enter, offering to pay my entry fee. Ginny organised for me to get a handicap rating quickly for *Stella-r*. A handicap rating, based on the displacement of the boat and its sail area, is a time factor multiplied to one's duration of the race, to make all boats have an even chance of winning.

All that was left for me to do on *Stella-r* was tidy up and put provisions on board. The race, about 150 miles, would be a good testing ground for my repairs. Fifty boats entered. I had a good start among several boats bigger than mine. With very little breeze, the lighter boats were faster. Many boats retired because there was not enough wind. It took a long time to complete the course. I was the second boat over the finish line and the second on handicap.

August had come and the first tropical storms had hit the Caribbean. Several competitors had sailed there to spend the winter cruising in warm water. I was tempted to follow, but Newport was too pleasant. The company, a marina berth at no charge and encouragement from club members to stay, made facing the Atlantic much harder. I also wanted to see the Newport Jazz festival, which was enjoyable.

Sadly the day arrived when I had to say goodbye. I was invited to a dinner where the club presented me with a proclamation and a club burgee for my contribution to their efforts in sailing.

The afternoon when I set sail, as I passed the club, their burgee was dipped and three cannons were fired to send me on safely. Three Twelve Meters class racing yachts used over several decades to win the America's Cup, led by *Waverly*, escorted me as far as Fort Adams.

This farewell was comparable to the farewell I was given in Galway in May.

***

I planned to leave on the afternoon tide when the lock gates opened. Late morning I went down to stow my last belongings, to find the boat outside the gates, alongside the *Pride of Galway*. Her crew had shifted my boat, with the help of some crew from the *Asgard 2*. The *Pride* and the *Asgard 2* had sailed over from the east coast to see me off.

I had a long lunch with Paddy, Rosie and John. Jim Fahy tracked me down on John's mobile phone, to stress that I should be at the boat by 16:00, because he was going to be down with a film crew. He wanted the boats in the bay by 16:30 since he had arranged with the marine rescue helicopter to pick him and the camera crew up to get aerial footage of the boat sailing off.

I had invited a number of friends, including Mayor Michael Leahy, to sail out aboard the *Pride*. John Killeen joined me aboard *Stella-r*. Before I turned towards the Atlantic, he would transfer to the *Pride*. When I arrived at the harbour, I was amazed at the size of the crowd that had gathered to bid me farewell. There were musicians playing traditional Irish music aboard the *Pride*.

Bidding my friends farewell was difficult. I had arrived in Galway as a stranger, with a damaged boat, and no money. I was leaving eighteen months later as an adopted son. I set sail with pride, and with the dream alive again.

The sports editor, Linley MacKenzie, of a free community newspaper, The Galway Advertiser, picked up on the story of the two South Africans sailing for Galway. One was black, the other white, but both were united by the sea and had mutual respect and admiration for each other. The skipper of the *Pride of Galway*, Shawn Cullens, was a fellow South African; he lived 7km from my parents. When we met in Galway the previous day, he passed on his father's regards. It was coincidental that I knew his father. Shawn had come to Ireland to visit relatives and stayed when offered a job in Dublin to skipper the sail-training vessel.

In the bay, I was joined by the *Pride*, the *Asgard 2* and a 24-foot yacht, *Enigma*. The helicopter came in low, with the television crew filming. John was below deck so that it appeared that I was alone on the boat. Suddenly, I was caught in the chopper's down draught. The wind increased from ten knots to forty knots. I rapidly released the mainsheet to spill the wind out of the sail, but a fitting was torn off the deck. It gave us all a fright, but no other damage was done.

After the crew had finished filming, I sailed over towards the *Pride* to put John aboard. She had dropped all her sails, bar her staysail to steady the boat. She steamed at an angle towards the wind on a course that I could sail. I sailed to her lee, bringing *Stella-r* two foot off her beam, to let John jump aboard. As his feet left my boat, I bore away from the *Pride*.

I gybed and headed off with a heavy heart. The *Asgard 2* came motoring up to me. When she was abeam, Barry Martin, the bosun, fired several guns in salute, then sailed towards the harbour. I was alone.

The *Pride* called on the VHF radio to say good-bye. While I was talking to John, I thought I heard a voice outside calling me. I looked out of the hatch, but saw no boat, putting it down to my imagination. The radio crackled again with another vessel calling. While we were speaking, I distinctly heard my name being called twice.

I went back up on deck and looked around. There was no sign of another vessel. Then the voice called once more. In the water something orange was coming towards me. It was just visible as I altered course and sailed towards it. It was Paddy in his kayak.

Paddy had missed the *Pride*, had charged home to load his kayak and had paddled five miles into the middle of the bay just to say good-bye.

'You were down below sleeping already,' he joked. 'With no windows, it's like a mole's tunnel, where you can't see me coming, nor the rocks, as you feel you way into your burrow!'

I liked to sleep when ashore. Paddie could tease me, and I would get him back later. We would go out together and say things to each other that others could not get away with.

It was a pleasant sail to Plymouth, and I got there in three days. A fishing boat towed me to Queen Anne's Battery where a few boats had already gathered. I was ten days early, but had several jobs to do before the safety inspection. There was a festive atmosphere. New friendships were formed. One in particular was with an American, Jack Gansel of *Amber 2*. Each late afternoon, he came over to have a drink aboard *Stella-r*.

The weekend after my arrival, Tim and Bram Halford arrived in Plymouth from their on holiday apartment in Cornwall. We went to lunch where the subject of birthdays came up. Bram asked when mine was. It was a week away. Laughing, they asked what I wanted for my birthday. Jokingly I said a spinnaker in a sock. They looked at each other, smiled and said fine. Tim took out his chequebook and asked how much it would cost. I was a little embarrassed, saying that it was very expensive.

'How much?' Tim insisted.

'Its about £1,000, so put your chequebook away.'

But Tim wrote me a cheque for the amount and gave it to me. Bram said that blue and yellow were her favourite colours, and that I could put my slogan on it.

I had no spinnaker, and intended to go racing without one. Tim explained to me that a business venture had gone well and that he wanted me to have something special from him and Bram, and the first spinnaker on the boat would please him. It was a lovely gesture.

I rang up several British sailmakers, but they could not guarantee me a delivery before the start, so I rang up a sailmaker in Cape Town, who promised to have the sail with me on time.

I passed the inspection, but still had jobs to do, when on 3 June, four days before the start, friends began arriving on *Stella-r* one at a time. They came down to the saloon where I was working on my battery power bank. I continued to clean terminals and check water levels in the cells, as we chatted. Soon the saloon was getting crowded. I felt a little agitated, but since these were my friends, I said nothing.

Cans of beers that they had brought were opened. Everyone was settling down to have a party. Many more friends were on the deck. Harry Mitchell from *Mitak* wanted a photograph of me on deck. When I came up, everybody except Harry and his wife went below. After the photo, we were summoned to the saloon. Rosie, who had come over a few days before, held a huge chocolate cake with twenty-five candles lit. It was a conspiracy to give me a surprise birthday party.

The following day I went to Heathrow airport to fetch my spinnaker, which had been flown in by South African

Airways, courtesy of the company. I was given a lift down by explorer Rex Warner whom I had met in Cape Town on his Operation Neptune expedition which followed the route to Mossel Bay taken by the Portuguese sailor, Bartholomew Diaz. Diaz was the Portuguese explorer who had discovered the route from Europe to the Far East via the Cape of Good Hope in 1488.

A few nights later, Paddie flew in. He could only stay for the night, because his business was taking him to Japan. The *Pride of Galway* sailed over for the start and acted as my support boat.

Three days before the start, a fax arrived from the False Bay Yacht Club wishing me well; they had kept in touch with me over the months. Next came a fax from the Royal Cape Yacht Club, wishing me well, and a message from the South African Ocean Racing Trust, which had generously decided to send me £800. Their help was very welcome and I appreciate it.

The night before the race, Lizzy Jackson and two friends came up from London. I had planned an early night. Initially eight of us were going to dinner, but in the end, twenty-four, some who were around-the-world sailors like Robin Davies, Josh Hall and David Adam, and BOC chief executive Nigel Rowe, dined together. Hans Burwell from Monitor windvanes came over from California to check and modify my self-steering gear, while Clive Bartlett, who did the marketing of VC Systems anti-fouling was there to get the necessary photographs for promotions later. Dinner lasted till 01:00, leaving me only seven hours sleep.

On Sunday, 7 June 1992, the sky was clear with no sign of wind. I had a quiet breakfast and wandered down the dock, saying good-bye to friends and competitors.

At 10:00 I was towed out of the marina to where the *Pride* was waiting to tow me into the start area. She towed me alongside, so that I could come aboard to do my last radio interview with Lizzy Jackson for BBC. A gentle breeze from the south-east piped up. Strings of boats were still being towed out. The start area was out of bounds to spectator craft and vigilantly patrolled by the Royal Navy. Only support boats, while still towing entrants, were allowed in the area. An hour later, I made my final farewell and cast off.

Somewhere to the west was the *Pride* with my friends. I could hear Rosie and the others singing. My mind turned to sailing and the start. I trimmed sails going up to the committee boat to have a look at how the start line was set in relation to the wind. There were two starting areas, with a big naval ship in the centre, and smaller naval ships marking the ends. The eastern start was for multihulls, while the western end was for monohulls like the *Stella-r*. Both divisions were starting on the same cannon simultaneously.

Ten minutes before to the start, I set up my largest headsail, but did not hoist it. I decided to wait until one minute before the start gun. Those remaining nine minutes dragged out. A few competing boats were near me, and whatever tactics they executed, I copied, only doing it just a bit faster and a little better.

The gun was fired. Twenty seconds later I was over the line and charging towards America. I looked around for the tall masts of the *Pride*. She was the largest yacht among the hundreds of spectator craft. I was astounded by the amount of craft that were out to see us off, and the number of choppers circling about with cameramen dangling out of open doors.

As I skimmed under full sail towards the Eddystone Rocks, a mark on the course, the *Pride* was to starboard. She looked a spectacular sight, with people aloft in her rigging. She came over and stood off to lee, struggling to keep pace with me. The little breeze had freshened and soon the *Pride* was left astern. She radioed to tell me that she was turning back. I did not feel the same isolation as in Galway, because she was in view astern, still following when I expected her to be heading back. Besides, I was

143

racing. There were competitors to be caught and spectator craft to be avoided. When I next looked back, she was a long way astern, just beginning to gybe and head towards port.

When the Eddystone Rocks loomed up ahead, I prepared to put up the spinnaker. Several boats surrounded me, with power boats zooming around taking television footage and photographs. Two helicopters came in close to get aerial shots. As I rounded the Eddystone, the spinnaker went up. *Stella-r* accelerated.

Start of the OSTAR in Plymouth.
Photographer: Clive Bartlett

Next stop USA.
Photographer: Clive Bartlett

One of the choppers did not anticipate my surge in speed. The pilot panicked as my boat threatened to pluck him out of the sky. He rapidly retreated, going backwards and up. The down draft from his rotors affected the air flow over my sails, collapsing the spinnaker. The second chopper must have taken some interesting shots, which were being broadcast live in France.

As the afternoon passed, the wind died. The spectator fleet began going home one at a time. Soon, it was only the racing fleet that was noticeable. The tide had turned against us. It was a struggle to keep the spinnaker full and drawing. I chose to sail inshore in search of less tide and better breeze.

At sunset I was off the southernmost point of Britain, Lizard Point, when the fog rolled in. It was a terrifying night. Ferries and shipping flew past at breathtaking speeds. I could hear their engines and horns sounding, and at times could see their deck lights as they came close. I was constantly on my radio giving my position and informing shipping that I was becalmed and unable to take collision avoidance action. By morning I had sailed only twelve miles. The breeze finally materialised and I was able to get the spinnaker flying properly. Close inshore were several boats which had decided to go north of the Scilly Isles. I chose to pass south around the Bishop Rock lighthouse in company with Italy's Franco Manzoli on *Alberobello by velscaf*. The wind freshened to the point that neither of us could handle spinnakers, but I was not going to take mine down first.

Late that afternoon, 140 miles from Land's End, I heard a loud thump on the bow. I felt the boat momentarily slow down and I charged up from the chart table to see a large plank drifting in my wake. I inspected the bow but could not see any damage. I continued to push the boat hard, as the wind went from south-east to north-west.

During that night, the competitors hit the first gale. The seas become mountainous. The boats that chose to stay south of the great circle, the shortest distance to Newport, were hardest hit. I encountered big waves breaking over the bow as *Stella-r* punched into the wind and seas under staysail and two reefs in the mainsail. The speed was good, but the motion of the boat was very uncomfortable. The sound of the gale was disturbingly audible below. *Stella-r* would rise up over a crest, then slam down into the trough. The whole boat shuddered.

Every six hours *Stella-r* needed her bilge pumped dry. After I had done this, I decided to get into a bunk for an hour, but the slamming was so bad that I could not sleep easily. I dozed in fitful bursts, but remained aware of the bucking of the boat. Suddenly I was rudely awaken by the sound of water in the bilge. I jumped up to find a tremendous amount in the bilge, sloshing up over the lee floorboards.

In my thermal underwear, I pumped the bilge from within the shelter of the cabin. Less than three minutes later, the same amount of water was back. Again I pumped it out, exhausted by the hard work. Immediately I checked the sea water intake for the water ballast tanks, followed by the keel bolts. No water was coming in there, but already the bilge was in need of pumping again. Thereafter I began a systematic search of the hull for the source of the water, between sessions of manning the pump.

My heart was racing. The leak had to be found and stopped. The nearest shore was a long way away, and at the rate of water coming in, I would not be able to sail, rest and keep enough water out of the boat for it to remain afloat. The weather appeared to be deteriorating. A third reef was needed. *Stella-r* was pounding harder. The motion below was tumultuous and moving about the interior became extremely difficult. I felt as if I was inside a washing machine.

In the area forward of the main bulkhead, on the port side, I detected the leak when I saw water spout from among damaged wooden veneers as *Stella-r* crashed over a wave crest. Immediately, without foul weather gear, a safety harness or boots, I charged up on deck to put the third reef in. The motion was slightly easier, but still *Stella-r* was pounding unmercifully. When I realised that my personal safety was in jeopardy without proper gear on, I returned below to clothe myself better, and returned to deck with a flashlight. Looking over the side on my hands and knees, drenched by waves washing over the deck, I saw an area of fibreglass about half a square metre delaminated from the wooden hull. I was not in a position to assess the full extent of the damage.

The harm was too severe to continue over two thousand miles to Newport. There was no time to question the causes, only to remedy a deteriorating situation. I tacked *Stella-r* onto port to lift the damage out of the water. Below deck, the water ceased to come in.

Poring over the chart, I weighed up my options. The Scilly Isles were the closest port, but with no engine nor detailed charts of those waters, sailing between the islands in strong tidal conditions was too risky. Next closest was Cornwall in England and Cork in Ireland was third. If I eased my sails and bore away to the north-east, I could reach Ireland on one tack provided the wind direction remained the same. In Ireland I was guaranteed help. It was the logical place to return to if I was to try to remain in the race.

Ahead lay 210 miles to Cork. On my new heading, the speed increased to seven knots and the motion was pleasant. With dawn the wind began to ease, followed by a shift in direction which enabled me to hoist a spinnaker. I was able to maintain the same speed, until twenty hours later when the wind dropped so much that I needed a full mainsail. It took me thirty hours to sight Mizen Head. I considered going into Kinsale, still sixty miles away.

In the late morning, I was able to put a phone call to John Killeen via Valentia radio. He suggested that I make for Baltimore and that he would see what could be done to get me back into the race as rapidly as possible. Immediately after that conversation which was overheard by anyone monitoring the frequency, Valentia asked me for details of my situation and for my position. They asked me to call in to them every half-hour with my updated position. I felt it unnecessary as I was in no imminent danger, but I co-operated.

Two hours later they had a phone call for me from Jim Fahy. He informed me that John was dispatching Pete with tools and material, but wanted to know the full extent of the damage. I had discovered that a weld on the space frame was broken, and asked that Pete bring a length of aluminium angle with him.

Ten miles off Baltimore, I was called up by the *LE Cura*, the smallest naval ship in the five-strong Irish fleet. She was on exercise with the rest of the Irish naval fleet in the area, and had been dispatched to stand by. I thanked the captain, assuring him that it was unnecessary. The wind had decreased considerably and my biggest fear was running out of wind before reaching the harbour, but he insisted on remaining.

The *LE Cura* took up station astern of me, launching her searider with an officer and two seaman. I was unable to allow anyone aboard until I was within a mile of the harbour because officially I was racing. Once that distance was achieved, the officer came aboard and the searider took me in tow. The sky was a brilliant blue. It was warm and there was not a breath of wind inside the beautiful natural harbour, when I docked at 17:00.

On shore I rang race control to advise them of my situation and location, telling them that I had no intention of retiring. Then I made inquiries about a boat builder because there was a boatyard in the town. The yard was closed, but I learnt that a Mr Dermot Kennedy had tools. He was out, but a message was left with his wife. I began to remove all the gear from the bow area so that I could assess the damage. It looked worse than it was. The space frame could be bolted together, and the hull fibre glassed over.

At 20:00 Pete McDonagh arrived, bringing Rosie and Mary O'Donnell along to help. They were all employed in good jobs, but had dropped whatever they were doing, and had told their bosses that they were off to help a friend in dire need. They had driven four hours to meet me. When they arrived, I learnt that Pete, Enda, Marcus and Peter Clinton had flown over to the start, only to be delayed in Dublin by fog. They missed me by an hour. Rosie teased me that I did not have to come to Ireland to say good-bye to the lads.

An hour later Dermot Kennedy arrived. There was not much he could do except lend us some tools and introduce me to Liam Hegarty, a local boatbuilder. He disappeared to track down Liam. While waiting, Pete and I put a plan into action to repair the broken aluminium limb. We had to cut a top opening into it. Without an angle grinder, he drilled abundant holes close together with a smallish bit and then used a larger one to join the holes, thus creating an opening large enough to put ones hand in to hold bolts with a wrench when tightening. It was painful work, cutting my hands several times on the jagged edges.

The girls shifted all the gear we had moved into the saloon onto the deck. Well after midnight Dermot returned with Liam, whose heavy Cork accent I had difficulty following. He took a quick look at the hull, saying that I had to get the boat up against the slipway to dry out while he got his partner and material. He promised to return by 03:00. With Dermot's punt we towed *Stella-r* to the slipway at high tide and secured her. Fortunately for me, the tidal range and times were in my favour.

Tiredness began catching up with me. Once *Stella-r* was aground and settled with nothing more that we could do, Pete and I turned into bunks while the girls went to Dermot's home; he had kindly offered them beds, to sleep.

It was a fitful sleep until Liam and his helper arrived. They began on the inside by sanding down the hull. When the sun rose, exposing the damage to its heat, the tide was nearly out. As the wood dried, the morning promised a warm day. I thought of my competitors three days ahead, racing on away from me. The weather would enable them to hoist their spinnakers.

Repairing damage in Baltimore
Photographer: Neal Peterson

Once the wood was dry enough, the boatbuilders sanded down the outside to expose a wider area to the sun's rays and then continued on the inside. Pete and I made up angle sections so that, when they were outside, we could work inside, out of their way. It was late morning on the turn of the tide that the two Cork men began fibre-glassing the exterior delamination. They used a rapid-drying hardener in the resin and soon were using a filler to get the exterior shape right.

It did not take the media long to track me down. Close to the harbour was a phone box. Various newspapers and radio stations contacted me there for my story. RTE had a film crew come down from Cork to interview Pete and me. Every few hours I gave the local radio an update of progress. Pete and the guys were great in that they did not mind me getting away from the boat to do those things. I assured the public that for me the race was far from over.

The tide refloated *Stella-r*. We towed her back to the main quay. The interior was ready to begin fibre glassing. The two men worked skilfully. It was sweltering hot, curing the fibreglass rapidly. The fumes that came off it were lethal. Frequently Liam and his assistant had to come out of the close confines for a breath of fresh air. Pete and I would go in to bolt the frame further together.

Eventually at 17:00, the fibre glassing job was done. When I offered payment, Liam gave me a bill of £80 which only covered material that he had bought. He would not give me a bill for their labour, saying that it was their contribution to my challenge. A special thanks to all those who helped get me back onto the water.

I felt suddenly alone and tired. It was arranged for a fishing boat to tow me out at midnight. I took advantage of the break to have a snooze. Near midnight the fibreglass was more than touch dry. The weather forecast was for light south-easterlies. I decided it was time to go. I was back in the race after a thirty-one hour pit stop.

With full sail up under spinnaker, I was ghosting along very slowly. During the day the wind died and I spent the evening watching the Fastnet Rock flash. Another day had gone by before I was back where the damage was discovered. It was sixty-seven hours later, I was 550 miles behind the class leader, Simon van Hargen on *Seatalk*, but I was back in the race.

For a week the weather was warm and sunny. The wind went west and the spinnaker had to come down, but the seas were gentle as I beat into the Atlantic swell. The electronic autopilot kept giving me trouble, and eventually ceased working. I relied on my Monitor windvane to steer me towards the Grand Banks, and then the finish.

After the Portishead radio broadcast, I plotted my position from the navigation aid on a chart. I counted the miles left to the finish. Some 1,350 miles lay ahead before I could realise my childhood dream. Nothing was going to stop me.

10

CATCH A FALLING STAR

My voyage from Newport to Ireland was hindered by bad weather. A week into the Atlantic, gusts reached 40 knots, creating a horrible cresting sea. I took down the mainsail and spent six days under number 3 genoa and staysail. Then five more days were endured sailing with only a staysail set.

My Monitor windvane coped very well, leaving me time to read a play by Bernard Shaw. It was extremely cold and I was grateful not to be constantly on deck.

On 2 September 1992 I came onto the continental shelf, where the sea floor rises from several miles deep to a couple of hundred feet. The wind increased, as did the size of the sea. The staysail was replaced with the storm jib. The daily average mileage did not drop significantly, and I was doing 150 to 160 miles a day. *Stella-r* continued to surf down the faces of the waves.

Twenty days after departing Newport, when I sailed onto the Porcupine Banks, 200 miles off Ireland's west coast, the seas became much steeper and from several directions simultaneously. I spent a lot of time below deck. Suddenly I tossed in my bunk upside down, with clothes and books from beneath the bunk piled on top of me. *Stella-r* was knocked down. The mast was forced into the water at an angle of about 100 degrees. It stayed there for a long time before *Stella-r* corrected herself and continued as if nothing had happened.

There was no noticeable damage on deck, but later that night I discovered that I had no navigation lights and my wind instruments had stopped working. They had been removed from the masthead. Miraculously, my VHF antenna was still there, enabling me to use the radio.

Soon I began receiving weather bulletins from Shannon radio, who were forecasting force 9 gales. I was encountering gusts of 55 miles per hour. It was not long before I was across the Porcupine Banks and into a more regular sea. That night I sighted Slyne Head lighthouse and, before dawn, the lights on the northern shore of the Aran Islands.

By early morning I was able to use the radio to call three friends. The high tide at Galway harbour was in early that afternoon. At the speed I was travelling, after a twenty-one day crossing from Newport, I would be there by late morning, before the harbour gates had opened. I chose to sail into the shelter of the Aran Islands and drop sail so that I could clean up the boat and myself.

Just after the lock gates had opened, I sailed up the channel with three reefs in the mainsail, a staysail and storm jib. My windvane steered the boat while I handled the sails. Once I had entered the harbour, I rapidly lowered the sails, and dropped two metal buckets filled with water over the side, acting as brakes to slow down the boat.

Peter McDonagh was on the dock to take my lines. Linley MacKenzie soon arrived to get the story of my twenty-one day crossing. She had saved the front page of the weekly *Galway Advertiser* for my homecoming. Peter Clinton was not long in joining my party, followed by John. Coincidentally, my arrival in the harbour was exactly twelve months to the day since I had first come to Galway under tow from the *LE Orla*.

I had caught my falling star and had realised my dream. But soon the restlessness began to creep up on me. I was constantly asked what my next adventure would be.

I travelled regularly to Dublin with John Killeen. I was researching businesses who could potentially sponsor me. One day while waiting for John in Dublin, I was walking down Baggot Street when I saw the name Airtime, an advertising, sponsorship and promotions business. I promptly walked in and made an appointment to see the managing director, Don Harris.

I explained my interest in young people and promoting environmental education through sport. Don was fascinated by my story and how I had used education to realise my racing dreams, creating my sailing career. After lengthy discussions, Airtime helped organise an extensive lecture tour of schools and clubs and began hunting for sponsorship for the Round Britain and Ireland race.

Winter came. I stayed for a while at Paddie's home. One morning in October, there was a knock at the front door. It was Gwen Wilkinson, the pretty girl that I had met when I was lecturing in a Galway hotel. She had called on me at the boat once before, but I was surprised by her visit to the house. I was busy on my computer upstairs finishing a chapter of this book, so I gave her a sailing video. An hour later I watched the end of the video with her and we began dating. I found out that it had been Gwen who had written the anonymous note.

In January 1993 I returned to London to the Earl's Court Boat Show, to find on the VC Systems stand a lovely photo of myself and *Stella-r* on the starting line. I was considering my next challenge. There was a possibility of using Allen Wynne-Thomas's 60-footer, *Cardiff Discovery*, for the Teeside Round Britain and Ireland Race and then the BOC Alone Around the World race. I need gear and sponsorship. VC Systems agreed to commit themselves to the challenge, sponsoring anti-fouling for a second campaign. I tried to get Henri Lloyd involved again, but they were not enthusiastic.

Feeling disappointed, I walked into Petra Stuart-Hunt's promotions office and asked her if she could set up a meeting with her client, the foul weather manufactures, Douglas Gill. Six weeks later we reached an agreement. It was a successful move as the support from Douglas Gill was not only clothing, but publicity support. Over the following year, their team was most helpful.

I had an extremely busy late winter and early spring lecture tour which took me from Galway all over Ireland to areas covering Counties Dublin, Cork, Offaly and Mayo. In February I sailed *Stella-r* to Dublin, with help from Eugene Waters, for the Dublin Boat Show. A New Zealander whom I met in late 1992 through John, Marc Grisé, joined me on my stand at the show, marketing my name and short-handed racing. Marc was a prime candidate to crew for me on the two-handed Round Britain and Ireland race.

After the Dublin show, I was invited to show *Stella-r* at the inaugural Kinsale Boat Show. In Kinsale, the Garda local youth liaison officer drove me to all the schools in the area where I spoke to pupils about the need to have dreams and how they could use their schooling to help them achieve those dreams. I also gave a series of slide lectures at the boat show on sailing, diving and pollution within the marine environment.

I had hoped that I would find contacts for obtaining sponsorship at the two boat shows, but nothing positive materialised.

Over a five-month period I lectured in some thirty venues, reaching an audience of about 5,000 people, mainly primary school children. Brona Cusack in Airtime set up and co-ordinated most of my lecture schedules. The most interesting series I gave was in Portloaise prison. This is a maximum security prison where most people confined are serving sentences for subversive crimes. The prison also accommodates prisoners on the non-subversive category who are located in a separate wing of the prison. The groups I addressed have an educational programme. There are five full-time teachers and a principal, assisted by twenty part-time teachers, some of whom have other teaching duties in the surrounding area. Prisoners in the subversive category will not associate or share facilities with other inmates and have to be accommodated in separate locations within the prison.

Two groups of non-subversive prisoners were allowed outside the cell blocks to me in prefabricated rooms, but within the prison grounds. These men were common criminals sentenced for non-subversive crimes who had been transferred from other prisons to work in Portloaise, thus getting additional remission of their sentences, since subversive prisoners are exempt from work duties for security reasons.

It was difficult talking to them at first. I was uncomfortable and did not want to be left alone. But after they had cracked a few jokes with me, I felt more at ease. At the end of those two lectures, I was given lunch in the staff canteen. It was a good meal. Afterwards I went into the cellblock to meet the men who had made headlines around the world for their destructiveness.

I spoke to five groups who had sentences ranging from ten years to life. All the prisoners were in normal everyday dress. They did not appear to be hostile towards the prison officers. I was given a warm reception by both prisoners and prison staff.

I had a captive audience indeed, my lectures were to have lasted an hour, but ran to two hours with penetrating questions from the inmates. There were several political questions about my life in South Africa, but mostly it was about how I dealt with the prolonged isolation, my fears and difficulties, and the reasons for the challenge. In many ways they could identify with me. Robin Knox-Johnston, a fellow single-handed sailor, commented after his 303-day non-stop voyage around the world in 1968, that to spend several months at sea, alone in a small boat, was worse than the same period in prison, sentenced to hard labour.

Looking at these men, it was hard to believe that they had masterminded acts of violence. They were ordinary human beings, who could have been sitting with one in a pul. Some might even have baby-sat someone's children. I did not feel at all threatened.

When I lecture I find distinct differences between various people. The more affluent the area the kids come from, the less interested they are, and the shorter their attention span. The ages of the groups determine the number and quality of the questions. The younger the group, the more keen they are at making comments, contributions or asking questions. Teenagers are the slowest group to get any response or questions from. The men in Portloaise prison had the vigour and curiosity of the younger people I had lectured to, but the depth and intellect of well-read adults.

When April arrived, there were no sponsors aboard for the Round Britain and Ireland race, and I could not pursue my idea of racing a 60-foot yacht. The Irish economy was still in recession, and companies were cautious about how they spent their funds. Three days before the close of entries for the Round Britain and Ireland race, I decided to enter *Stella-r* instead.

When Airtime realised my disappointment at the lack of financial support, they contributed to my campaign, covering the entry fee and leaving me some money for provisions. I made them a sub-sponsor of my challenge, putting their name on the hull beside Douglas Gill, VC Systems and other sponsors.

In mid-June I began writing a newspaper column for the *Galway Advertiser*. A week later Marc Grisé flew in, and after a few days' preparation, we set sail for Plymouth. Marc and I spent several days in Plymouth before the fourth of July start to acquaint ourselves with some of our fellow competitors and to do one final detailed check over the boat.

Several rivals from the transatlantic race were taking part again. Competition in our class was once more from Simon van Hargen in *Seatalk*. Marc and I decided that we were not on the starting line to win, but to finish and enjoy the race.

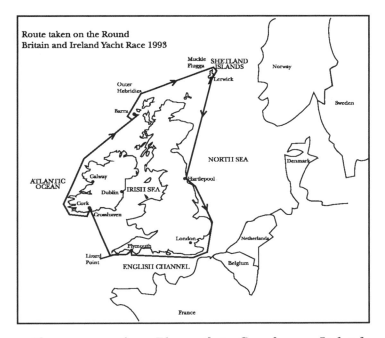

Route taken on the Round
Britain and Ireland Yacht Race 1993

The race was from Plymouth to Crosshaven, Ireland, then on to Barra in the Hebrides, Lerwick, the main port of the Shetlands, with Hartlepool in Teeside the last stopover before the return to Plymouth. All islands and rocks, except for the Channel Islands, were to be left to starboard. Fifty-eight boats had entered, but only fifty-two boats, representing eight nations, made it to the starting line in Plymouth Sound. The British had the most competitors, followed by the Dutch with nine boats. All the French could muster was one boat.

I sported a long mop of curly hair before the race. Marc volunteered to have his hair cut off for child leukaemia, and tried to talk me into doing the same. When I showed little interest, two friends decided that it was going to be done. They sat me down and asked me to name my favourite charity. The Royal Naval Lifeboat Institution was my answer.

I had bigger worries than having an involuntary haircut. I needed money to pay for my liability insurance and a contingency fund. Unable to find financial help, I turned to my close friends. Don Harris of Airtime again offered me some help and I decided to switch my campaign to sail under the Irish flag because all the help I had received to get to the start line had been Irish. There were no Irish entrants.

To keep busy and psychologically worry my competitors, I began to drill hundreds of holes in the bunkboards. I wanted to improve ventilation beneath the mattresses, and make the boards lighter and more manageable when they were lifted to get into the storage areas. My competitors saw it as an extreme way of lightening the boat and concluded that victory was all-important.

On the Friday night before the start, I had agreed to have my hair cut by Chris Briggs who had sailed with me the previous year. He had built a radical machine, *Maverick*, for the 1993 Round Britain. Chris believed that if I was to beat his 30-foot boat, I needed to reduce weight and windage aloft. He became my barber. It was well publicised in the marina that the proceeds raised would go to the lifeboat. Barry Sullivan of Pentaneous Insurance agreed to sponsor my liability insurance. My head felt very cold at the start of the race.

Ninety-seven pounds was raised, but this did cause me one difficult situation because Clive Bartlett had to take publicity photographs for the Douglas Gill catalogue, and my baldness looked strange. We tried it with a cap, but that did not work. Fortunately, there was an old picture that they were able to use, taken in the Douglas Gill gear. This beginning was different to the transatlantic start in that we commenced from inside the breakwater and had to sail a lap around the harbour before heading for the Eddystone Rocks. There was a collision on the start line when the new *Mercury Messaging* crashed into *Global*

Challenger losing her bow sprit. We sailed well, getting out of the sound before the wind died, becalming half the fleet.

Neal and Marc set sail.

Mark Gatehouse on *Queen Anne's Battery*, a local yachtsman from Plymouth who had done several transatlantic and Round Britain races, touched the Eddystone Rocks. He rounded too close, but fortunately no damage was done.

Magic Machine was a beautiful 45-foot Dutch aluminium cruising yacht. Every one envied Richard Everdij and Adriaan Valen. She passed us at the Lizard having followed *Stella-r* inshore to get out of the tide. The wind was fresh at the Bishop Rock. By the time we rounded, a nasty gale had developed. We helmed for most of that night, thinking of the guys on *Magic Machine* sitting in their slippers below deck while their autopilot steered them. Eventually I decided that this was an endurance race requiring the use of the Monitor.

By midday the next day, the system had passed and we were off the Kinsale gas fields with no wind, in the company of whales. We could not get *Stella-r* to move in the desired direction. The seas calmed down rapidly, but the small swell shook what wind we had out of the sails. It was then that *Maverick* came ghosting by. I was furious that we did not have the sponsorship to have a new and greater range of sails. I also wanted my hair back from Chris.

We had a close finish in Cork with a 49 footer, *Illaria*, sailed by a father and daughter team. She had chosen to go south during the blow, and appeared on the horizon the same distance as us from the finish line. There was a lovely breeze but a strong tide, short tacking the two boats. We beat them by fifteen seconds.

The same finish line was the start too. In each stopover every vessel had a mandatory forty-eight hours rest. Two days later, *Illaria* and *Stella-r* met again. Minutes before the start we hoisted sail. Marc killed the borrowed outboard engine. I asked him if the engine was fine on the bracket, wanting him to take it below, but he was so wound up with the start, he did not pay attention. When I told him to get rid of it, he took it literally and dropped the engine accidentally overboard.

My morale followed the engine to the sea floor and remained there until Barra. It was a tough leg with more head winds and gales. It was too rough to cook. The deck was more often underwater than above as huge waves crashed over the bow, threatening to drag off anything that was not securely battened down. We were cold, wet and hungry. I could sea land twenty miles to the east. The hills around Galway were clearly noticeable as we crossed the head of Galway Bay. I felt depressed. There was no money in my bank account. I could not afford the loss of the engine, and it had to be replaced before the end of the race.

It was a relief to get to Barra in the Outer Hebrides. We sailed in onto a mooring along side *Modi Khola*, a 30-footer that had beaten us in by a fair margin. She was not a new boat, and of the same construction as *Stella-r*. What made her such a fast boat was a mystery. Skipper Chris Shepherd was in a bad way, with saltwater sores on his arms and thighs, with skin so raw and painful that he needed medical attention. He spoke of coming below deck shaking not from the cold, but from his deteriorating physical condition.

Another skipper to need medical attention was Kitty Hampton on *ROC*. She slipped on deck and had dislocated her knee. Hansuelie Albrecht, an orthopaedic surgeon on arch-rival *Ours De Berne*, less than an hour ahead of *ROC*, took one look at Kitty and told her to get off the leg. He had none of the tools of his trade on holiday with him, but got the local doctor to strap Kitty's leg up. Both doctors were of the same opinion that continuing could cause serious complications, but Kitty continued to race, shadowing *Ours De Berne*.

Raspa, sailed by Jan Valstar and Walter Kubold was in ahead of us, much to my surprise. The rivalry was so fierce and the friendships so good, that we professed not to be talking to each other ashore. Karl Beer and his son, Roderick on *Jane-Air*, followed us by several hours. They had had an extremely bad passage having lost battery power. In the gales their morale had sunken so low that they stopped sailing for eighteen hours and went to bed.

Two days out on the third leg to Lerwick, we sighted *Raspa*. Several times we spoke on the radio, although we had lost sight of each other at sunset. Off the south western Shetlands I spotted another yacht sporting hi-tech sails sailing past us on the edge of poor visibility. It was not *Raspa*, but later turned out to be *Victoire*, another 30-foot Dutch entry. At daybreak the next morning we tacked inshore. *Raspa* spotted us doing it and called us up to say that we were going the wrong way and that he would not follow us. They had hoped that by going separate directions, we would not get an advantage over them. We went inshore looking for wind as the fresh breeze showed signs of dying away.

We rounded Muckle Flugga, the northernmost tip of the British Isles and regarded as the notorious Cape Horn of the northern hemisphere for its severe weather. We were expecting gales. Instead, it was the frustrating calms. There was no sign of *Raspa*, but we did hear *Victoire* radioing in to say that they had rounded. We fought a strong current in very light breeze, eventually rounding two hours behind *Victoire*, and deliberately did not use the radio until we knew *Raspa's* location.

Once around, we put up a spinnaker. Marc was moody and I was frustrated. I remained on deck keeping the boat moving at a knot over the ground towards Lerwick. At the end of my watch, I deliberately did not call Marc for his watch. In his mood, I feared we would go backward with the current. Both of us were extremely tired and in need of a decent meal because we had run out of food. Being short of cash, I had not bought extra food, but had limited our purchases to basics. With only a few basic provisions, Marc had come up with some wonderful dishes during the race.

I sighted another vessel ahead of *Stella-r* on the horizon, but was not sure if it was *Raspa*. Three hours later, I sighted a second sail astern. They had set a spinnaker and caught some breeze. It was *Raspa*. Another race within the race had began. We had to get away from *Raspa* and catch the unidentified competitor.

We gybed into a fresh shore breeze. Again *Raspa* did not follow us. The boat ahead of us took its time to follow us, loosing valuable time as we narrowed the gap between us. The boat ahead was *Cuttlefish*, a new 35-foot boat built for the race. We closed the distance very quickly, and in no time put a mile between them and ourselves. Seeing us catch them so rapidly could not have helped their morale and we overtook them.

We sailed into the Shetlands to a hearty welcome. The coastguard observed us tacking very close inshore to stay in the breeze and so avoid a no-wind patch. I watched the depth instrument knowing that it was accurate, while I helmed. Marc stood by ready to handle sails at my call. When the depth reached 15 meters, we tacked away about a boat length from the ledges. The coastguard held their breath as they lost sight of us under the cliff, worried that we would go aground, but were relieved to see us come out safely, only to repeat the process several times.

An inflatable was at the line to meet us as we sailed into the tight harbour at 04:00. It was superb to have someone there at that hour of daybreak to handle our mooring lines, especially as we were under sail. Four hours later, *Raspa*, *Cuttlefish* and *Jane-Air* arrived. *Victoire* and *Alice's Mirror* were less than half an hour ahead.

What made Lerwick so special was that every boat was allocated to a host family to ensure that we enjoyed our stay. Soon our host, Ian Fraser, was down at the quay. He helped find me a replacement outboard engine. I did not have the funds to buy it, but was able to borrow it from a fellow sailor. Ian took us on a tour of the island, did our laundry, took us home twice for meals and helped with some of the repairs. When we left Barra, we encountered some heavy weather for a day. We bounced off a wave and cracked the forward bulkhead. Lerwick was the best port in the race by far, well worth all the agony it had taken to get there.

The fifth leg was uneventful, and we passed the North Sea oilfields in decent weather. For the first time there was warmth in the sun as we ran under spinnaker. Two hundred miles from Hartlepool we got a wind shift and had to drop the spinnaker. Hours later the wind altered again and up it went. We carried it a bit longer, predicting a wind shift which did not materialise and dropped the spinnaker. I was contemplating lowering genoa number one because we were nearly on its wind strength limit. I decided to leave it up and push harder. When Marc took over the watch, I told him that if the gusts increased to over 20 knots, to take it down. Two hours later Marc called me to say that we had blown the sail out. A gust of 25 knots had hit, ripping the top panel.

It was a long night. At day break the wind died and we ghosted along to windward with a small sail set. We were met again at the line by an inflatable boat which brought us a bottle of champagne.

Awaiting us ashore was a rather empty marina with *Jane-Air*, *Alice's Mirror* and *Victoire* already tied up. We had a free breakfast and a sleep.

Along with several other boats that needed sail repairs, we found the nearby sail loft a rip-off for the repair done. Teeside Development did what they could to make it a good stopover, providing free transport to get what we needed, but what I will always remember was being charged £60 for a lousy seam to be stitched back together which in an expensive sail loft would cost £30 maximum. To repair the torn sail, I had to sell my generator and camera.

This left me very depressed, but my fellow competitors lifted my spirits. The crews of *Raspa* and *Jane-Air* invited me to dinner at a Chinese restaurant where I forgot about sailing, while Marc went out drinking with two competitors.

The final leg was the toughest. We chased *Jane-Air*, *Victoire* and *Alice's Mirror*, who has started two hours ahead. It was a spinnaker start down the coast, in a lovely fresh breeze. The North Sea race from Hartlepool to the Netherlands started minutes before our start, giving us boats to chase and catch. Near Lowerstoft, the most easterly town in Britain, we crossed paths with *Alice's Mirror*. They tacked inshore of several sandbanks. Not having the detailed charts, we stayed outside the sandbanks. It was the last we saw of her.

In Dover Straits, the narrowest body of water between England and France, we dodged shipping as we fought our way into near gales and head winds. I was amazed at the amount of shipping we encountered in the Straits, some passing at speeds in excess of 15 knots.

We beat west in the English Channel heavily reefed to cross paths with *Jane-Air*. It was slow going and frustrating, especially as I had an appointment with Gwen and Don Harris at the finish line. Off Start Point, the wind died. The last thirty miles were even slower. In the early morning fog, I helmed.

We had lost sight of *Jane-Air* during the night, but sighted her off the breakwater in Plymouth a mile ahead. We were bringing the wind with us and looked as if we would catch her. But soon she got the breeze too, and shot away. They were a lighter boat, driven faster in the gentle airs than my boat. It was another hour before either of us was able to cross the Sound. *Jane-Air* beat us to the finish by twenty minutes, putting us fifth in our class. I felt disappointed, but having raced without a sponsor, forced to sell gear to keep going, sailing a home-built boat and with sails that have done more than 20,000 miles, it was an achievement to finish.

When the horn off the Royal Western Yacht Club was sounded, we ended a good but tough race. Unfortunately Don had business in London and could not wait. He had to catch the 08:30 train. I was disappointed, but that is what happens when one depends on the wind. We crossed the line at 08:29, to beat *Alice's Mirror*, *Victoire* and *Raspa*. At least when Gwen arrived, I was at the station to meet her.

Sadly we learnt that *Magic Machine*, a boat we envied for speed and comfortable sailing, had lost her keel and capsized in the English Channel. Both sailors were rescued and the boat was later salvaged.

Spud Spedding and Mervin Weekly on *Independent Freedom* finished in style three days later. They had done the race together several years before in a gaff-rigged boat. They had come last, but had had fun. Every evening at six, routinely they had happy hour. For the start and finish they dressed up as gentlemen. Since they were sailing a gentleman's pleasure cruiser, they were determined to look the part. At the entrance to Plymouth Sound, they spotted a capsized dingy. Without any debate, they turned about and rescued its four occupants.

When *La Gamine* finished during the middle of the night, I was on the dock to meet them with two cold beers. No one came down to meet us when we finished, and I made a point of meeting everyone, if I was around, with a beer. Walking to the clubhouse with the two brothers, veterans of the last race, Peter Rice asked his brother David if they would do it again. His reply was: 'Not next year, but in four years time I will have recovered.' They echoed my feelings. It is a great race, where one sees beautiful lands and wild life, and meets wonderful people among the competitors and on the stopovers. To finish is to be a winner. The trophies should be for those who came in last, after everybody else had left, but who had persevered.

EPILOGUE

In *Seven Pillars of Wisdom*, T.E. Lawrence stated that men dream, but not equally. He identified two kinds of dreamers: those who fantasize in the darkness, but awake to find that it was in vain, and then there is the formidable person, who dreams with open eyes by day. He strives to make his aspiration attainable.

I am of the latter kind. Chasing goals has never been easy, and to realise them takes courage. I rarely dreamt silently. It was through reading books about the sea, and the encouragement of my parents that I found strength to chase my desires. To fail was not to try at all.

There were always obstacles to circumvent. If everything was easy, there would be nothing to aspire to. When I did fall, getting up was hard, but it had to be done if I was going to cross an ocean single-handed. There has always been the love-hate relationship with the elements. Often in my life at sea I questioned why I was doing the things I chose. The answers were not always evident. When I had lost my rudder and my future looked very bleak, I had to draw on my inner strength. To venture into the unknown with limited resources was unnerving. Looking at my experiences and the friendships that developed over the years, I found the true wealth of my life, and feel I have matured.

So often I asked myself if I could financially afford to chase my dreams. The answer was no, yet I persevered, understanding that it would be a struggle. To be dedicated and single-minded about one's ambitions was the fuel that had helped me along when building *Stella-r*, and also when crossing the ocean. There are people who cashed in their life's savings to chase their dreams. This is not an escape from a past they do not like, but the realisation of a future they have conceived.

The tougher the challenges became, the more determined I grew. I love the sea and the spirit of adventure. It is what will keep me young. After sailing the Atlantic ocean single-handed three times in my beloved *Stella-r*, covering more than 15,000 miles, my appetite for adventure has grown and I have not looked back. When Marc joined me for the Teeside Round Britain and Ireland race, I did enjoy the race with him, but I also learnt that I am better suited to single-handed sailing. I love company, but on those blue waves alone, I have felt the feelings of inner peace that I have encountered nowhere else.

Gwen sailed with me over a thousand miles after the last race. She was the only girlfriend to live with me on my spartan boat with no heating, toilet or shower. She faced very much a situation of "Love me, love my boat". It has given me hope that one day when I choose to stop solo racing, that I will be able to cruise with my family and give them the opportunity to see the world through diverse experiences.

My boat is my home, the oceans of the world my country. No adventurer hangs up his or her sea boots for long. I would not allow weed to grow on *Stella-r's* hull. In July 1994, I will race solo from Falmouth, England to Charleston, South Carolina, in the inaugural BOC Transatlantic Challenge, and then in September 1994, compete in the 27,000 mile BOC Alone Around The World race, which starts in Charleston, calling in Cape Town, Sydney and Punta del Este before returning to Charleston some nine months later.

After I entered *Stella-r* in these races, last December with John Killeen's unfailing help, Gwen and I moved *Stella-r* to his shed in Oranmore, where, amidst all the work, we remained domicile on board. We could not afford to rent accommodation, and with a very small budget of £500 saved from lectures and work Gwen did, we lived frugally so that the few materials we had to buy, we could get.

With the voluntary help from the travelling community, namely Willie McDonagh and Paddy Donovan, from Hillside beside Castle Park, and Eugene Waters who has moved his fibre glassing business to Tara Pier in Kinvara, we significantly improved *Stella-r*. She has been lengthened by two feet in order to meet the BOC minimum size requirement of 40-foot, built twin retractable dagger boards in the stern to help with directional stability when sailing down wind, and put in two mandatory watertight bulkheads. We also paneled the interior and painted the hull and deck. Gwen created four large oil paintings in the saloon depicting scenes from Ireland.

In January, I returned to the London Boat Show, where VC-Systems anti-fouling renewed their support, but with additional paint supplied, is now known on board by the International Paint name, its sister company. Robertson Stowe, a part of the Simrad group, and Douglas Gill also returned for another season. Whale, the Northern Irish bilge pump manufacture, and Spinlock have supported me with products. Through Dublin's Western Marine, Marlow Rope gave me a significant discount on all my rope requirements. In Oranmore, many employees of Cold Chon, Coens, Steelforms and Eurotec Signs, the commercial graphic side of Municiple Equipment Company, have bent over backward to help.

Still without a financial sponsor, Robin Deacy helped me find patronage from Richard Burrows in Irish Distillers, with a budget for radar. In South Africa, now emerging economically from its post apartheid era, Graham Lizamore began the negotiations for a main sponsor. Afrox, a subsidiary of the BOC group, has helped Graham in his challenging task.

To all the individuals and companies who have helped me realise my varied goals, I wish to express my sincere thanks. But I want to say a very special thank you to my parents, and to John Killeen and Gwen Wilkinson who stood beside me day and night and gave me that extraordinary encouragement and strength to ensure that I succeed.

I spent an important part of my life in Ireland. Fate took me to there and introduced me to some wonderful people. It was there that some of my seeds sown in South Africa grew to produce fruit.

To those who have sat in their armchair and read my book, remember that I found my direction through reading, but it is up to the individual to realise his or her goal. Nothing is impossible.

GLOSSARY

beam   — The middle sides of a hull.

chain plates — Attachment points on the deck to which the shrouds connect.

Fo 'C' Sle — The point of the ship near the bow where the seamen live

genoa   — A large triangular shape sail.

GMT — Greenwich Mean Time.

GPS — Geographic Positioning System, which is used for constant updating of navigation data.

growler — A Canadian word to describe a large chunk of ice broken off from the main iceberg.

gybe — When sailing off the wind, to alter course so that the wind comes from the sternquater.

halliards — ropes used to hoist the sails.

shrouds — lengths of wire used to keep the mast incolumn.

space frame — a frame work structure within the vessel from which the rigging is attached, the mast sits on and the keel is bolted to.

spinnaker — the large colourful balloon like sail used to sail off the wind with.

spreader — horizontal supports attached perpendicularly to the mast, through which the rigging passes at the ends.

stantion — supports for the two wires which surround the boat to prevent the crew sliding overboard.

storm jib — a very small triangular sail used in storm wind conditions.

transom — the very back of the boat.

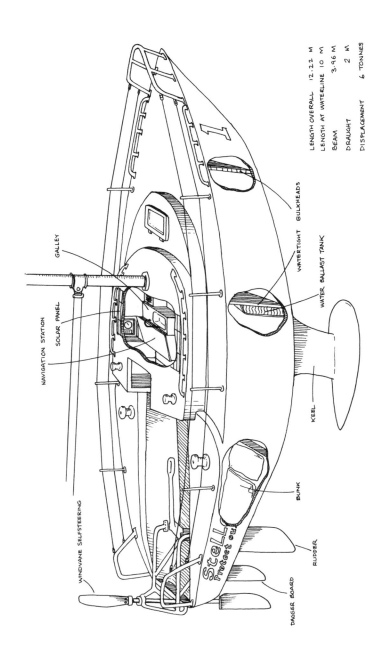

NAVIGATION STATION

SOLAR PANEL

GALLEY

WINDVANE SELFSTEERING

DAGGER BOARD

RUDDER

BUNK

KEEL

WATER BALLAST TANK

WATERTIGHT BULKHEADS

SteLL
Protect ou

LENGTH OVERALL   12.22 M
LENGTH AT WATERLINE 10 M
BEAM   3.96 M
DRAUGHT   2 M
DISPLACEMENT   6 TONNES

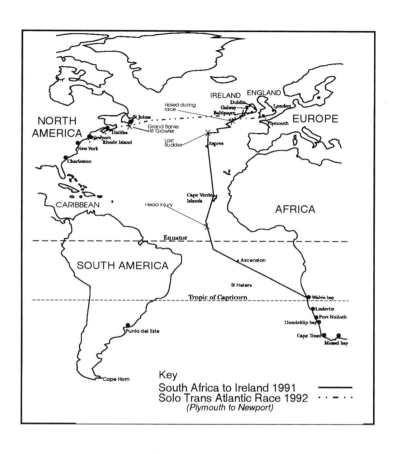

Key
South Africa to Ireland 1991 ——————
Solo Trans Atlantic Race 1992 · — · · —
(Plymouth to Newport)

DATES AND EVENTS

3 June 1967	— Born Capetown, South Africa
Autumn 1973	— Recovered from last hip operation
January 1980	— Began high school, followed by the up-rising
Summer 1980	— Started sailing and scuba diving
December 1984	— Graduated high school
January 1985	— Attended college in Los Angeles
January 1985	— Diving for diamonds
April 1987	— Studying and diving in Scotland
Autumn 1988	— Began constructing *Stella-r*
Summer 1989	— Delivered yacht to Caribbean
22 Nov 1990	— Launched *Stella-r*
10 Feb 1991	— Left Simonstown for Walvis Bay
2 June 1991	— Depart Walvis Bay for England
August 1991	— Rudder destroyed in collision
7 Sep 1991	— LE Orla tows *Stella-r* into Galway
October 1991	— Keel torn out of hull
January 1992	— Appeared on Kenny Live TV chat show
March 1992	— Mayor launched *Stella-r*
May 1992	— Left Galway for Transatlantic race
7 June 1992	— Start of Transatlantic race
8 June 1992	— Holed during race
6 July 1992	— Crossed finish line in Newport
August 1992	— Sailed back to Ireland
Winter 1992	— Irish Lecture tour
4 July 1993	— Started Round Britain and Ireland race
December 1993	— Entered BOC Alone Around the World race

ACKNOWLEDGEMENTS

I wish to thank the following people, companies and organisations who helped me make my career as a diver and yachtsman possible, and offered me assistance with this manuscript.

Malcolm Goodbody
Ronnie Robbins
John Killeen
Dermot O'Meara
Peter Clinton
Marcus Casey
Graham Lizamore
Sue Scholtz
David Knight
Arch Motors
Dr. Wim de Konig
Julia Humbertson
Mairead Keher
Tom Canny
Williem Kiely
Mr. P. Hurst — Jamerson and Green
Mike and Heather Edgar
Biscomm
Eircell
Spud Spedding
Marlow Ropes
Martin Carter
The Royal Cape Yacht Club
The Ocean racing Trust
False Bay Yacht Club
Gabriel King
Graham Smith
Afloat Magasine
Bandon radio
Galway Bay FM
Mike Sandover
Poolbeg Yacht Club
Des McWilliam
Tom McWilliam
Marc Grise
Denis and Robert Headon
Dr. Moosa Bhamjie
Mark Schrader

Tom McSweeny
David Branigan
Galway Maritime
Jimmy Kelly
Pat Rynn Engineering
Johnathan Williams
Don Harris
Airtime
Brona Cusack
Trevor Dabber
Jannie Reuvers
Brian and Marion Cole
North Sails — Cape Town Loft
Lt. Mark Mellet
Tim and Bram Halford
Atlantic Marine — Shawn Rogers
Dermot Kennedy
Liam Hegarty
Hollard Insurance
Gus Barret
Colm DeBarra
DeBeers of Shannon
Lizzie Jackson
Dennis Barrett
Andrew and Rose Brock
David Baynes
Rosie Coyne
Customs—Galway
Glendy Collins
Frank Sheridan
Dave Marcus
Michael Craughwell
Stevin Durkin
Cold Chon
Municiple Equipment Company
Robin Deasy
Des and Pattie Campbell
Peter Evans
Jim Fahy
Carl Flannery
Eamon Fox
Tim Gunning
Peter Green
Murphy's Brewery
Dr. Micheal Hynes
Kevin Hallinan
Dave Harvey

Midas productions
John Joseph
John Claustra
Brian Lynch and Associates
Mark Parkin
Roberston Stowe Marine
Mark Luffingham
Michael Leahy
Bobby Molloy T.D.
Linley McKenzie
Roger Martin
Peter McDonagh
The Met. Services
Ray McGrogan
Mary O'Donnel
Pat Orman
Enda and Susan O'Coineen
Neil Whorsiskey
Galway Rotary Club
John Coyle
Paul Ryan
Envision Marketing Consultants
John and Maureen Rabbit
Nan Rice
Mike Shaughnesay
John O'Shaughnessy
The Connaught Tribune
Vinnie and Neil McNeill
Eric Waller
Waller and Wickam
Dr. Albert Wilson
Seamus McNamara
Clive and Georgina Bartlett
Spinlock
Douglas Gill
Peta Stuart Hunt
Gwen, Paddy and Anne Wilkinson
Eugene Waters
Fibre Glass Engineering
Colin Farlem
Dr Lorry Leve
The BOC Group
Afrox
Arnold Cook
My teachers at Livingstone High school
Ian Wingate
Dewett Schonken

Queen Anne's Battery Marina
Thistle Park Tavern
Marinus Goulooze
Manex and Power Marine
Richard Peterson
Pat Fraser
Central Boating
Peter Kemp
Angelo Laveranos
Roger February
Clive Laybrant
Seamans Mission — Walvis Bay
Garmin GPS
International Paint
VC Systems
Whale Pumps
Steve Black
George Pyke
Bill and Mike Meusell
Tony Flaherty
The Crew of Le Orla
The crew of Le Cura
The crew of the *Girl Cleonia*
Shannon Marine Rescue Centre
The Aran Island Lifeboat Station
Steelforms
Coens — David Coen
Hans and Sylvia Burwell
Joe Cosgrove
Bret and Cosgrove Paint Centre
Michael Hern and Family
Liam and Jonathan Curan
Wesley O'Shaughnessy
Dave Heaney
Pascal Flaherty
Micheal O'Ceallaigh
Athlone Electrical Wholesalers
Enver Daniels
John Brant